THE MAN WHO WAS
JEKYLL AND HYDE

THE MAN WHO WAS JEKYLL AND HYDE

THE LIVES AND CRIMES OF DEACON BRODIE

RICK WILSON

The History Press

For Daisy and Corin

Cover image from Alamy

First published 2015

The History Press
The Mill, Brimscombe Port
Stroud, Gloucestershire, GL5 2QG
www.thehistorypress.co.uk

British Library Cataloguing in Publication Data.
A catalogue record for this book is available from the British Library.

ISBN 978 0 7509 6019 9

Typesetting and origination by The History Press
Printed in Great Britain

CONTENTS

ABOUT THE AUTHOR

Rick Wilson has been a magazine editor in London, Amsterdam
and Edinburgh, where he now lives with his wife Alison. He has
three children and five grandchildren. This is his seventh published
book. Previous titles by Rick Wilson:

The Amsterdam Silver
Scotland's Unsolved Mysteries
The Press Gang
Scots Who Made America
The Gemini Enigma
The Man Who Was Robinson Crusoe

ACKNOWLEDGEMENTS

Thank you to – Dutch writer Marco Daane for his insights on Deacon Brodie's Amsterdam arrest; antique journo Bill Sinclair for his antiquarian Edinburgh journals; Ian Nimmo, past chairman of the Robert Louis Stevenson Club, for all his borrowed knowledge; Edinburgh University's Owen Dudley Edwards for his thought-provoking views; Keith Walker, Napier University information services adviser, for his 'enlightening' help; tour leader Magnus Moodie for his Old Town guidance; David S. Forsyth, National Museums Scotland, for pointing me to Brodie's forged keys and dark lantern; and John and Felicitas Macfie for showing me around their house that once housed RLS.

INTRODUCTION

Who was Deacon Brodie? Many people profess to know the name, but a surprisingly large number are unsure if they know his story. Not to be smug about it: that number would have included this writer before embarking on this project.

The daytime William Brodie was a superficially charming gentleman and city councillor who commanded the timorous respect of fellow citizens as he went about his business of winning work for his cabinet-making company. Certain things about him, however, betrayed the fact that he was something more than a good, solid, upright Edinburgher. In what was a fairly grey-toned eighteenth-century Scotland he could seem like a bit of a dandy, with his cocked hat, flowered waistcoat and silver buckled top-quality shoes; not to mention a livid scar on one cheek – the result of a dispute over loaded dice in a card game. Even a stranger might have reckoned there was at least a boyish naughty streak there.

But it was far more serious than that. Despite showing occasional flashes of fatherly tenderness for favoured members of his five-strong illegitimate brood, he was basically a selfish and ungrateful soul with an insatiable appetite for money, who once said he would rather go to sea than develop the business left to him by his father –

along with a huge fortune – as he had seen that big treasure prizes were being taken by sailors of every rank. Nor was he grateful for his privileged position on the city council that, in the days before corruption as we now know it, afforded him, as deacon of wrights, an endless conveyor belt of business opportunities. These, crucially, included crime. For as his day job gave him access to clients' shops, houses and safe keys – from which he made copies – by night he morphed into a cloaked, sinister burglar who skulked around the closes of old Edinburgh with a dark lantern and darker intentions.

Eventually found guilty of a long series of robberies that had shocked and mystified the city's population, this was an extremely aberrant man who was to fall foul of his own greed and deep psychological complexities – including an enthusiasm for theatricality – that prompted him to become another person in the same body. So perhaps that should be persons, plural. By his own confession he was a 'very ingenuous fellow', but he was also a gambler, a spendthrift, a deceiver of two mistresses and generally – perhaps the biggest societal sin of this particular period – a betrayer of his own class and upbringing. Not for murder, but for this – as well as his audacious attempt to rob the Excise Office of Scotland – he and an accomplice were hanged on a scaffold said by some to have been designed by himself a year before.

But another piece of joinery figures large in his tale. One of his cabinets was to be the catalyst that 'fathered' Dr Jekyll and Mr Hyde in Edinburgh. A century after its creation in Brodie's workshop in the Lawnmarket, the cabinet stood at the foot of Robert Louis Stevenson's bed in the New Town, and the then-young author, reminded every day of its provenance, became so obsessed by the Brodie story – and thus by any human being's capacity to be more than one personality in one body – that he was moved to no fewer than three creations based on him. These were two plays and a horror-story novella that became an immediate bestseller and introduced the world to the character(s) whose names have figured ever since in everyday English speech.

Talking to the Museum of Edinburgh about details of William Brodie's life, including the family Bible from whose birth register all reference to him had been excised, we learned that in planning to mount an exhibition entitled 'Edinburgh, City of Stories' it had invited friends of the institution to vote for their favourite tale out of three – Burke and Hare, Greyfriars Bobby or Deacon Brodie. The vote went to Greyfriars Bobby, but surely its proponents were barking up the wrong tree? For as we were saying, if more people knew more about the Deacon, his remarkable tale would doubtless have easily swung the vote.

Why is it so remarkable? There are many reasons – because of the stark differences in his two personalities; because he eluded truth and justice for so long; because he was not all evil, having a gentler side for friends (and families); because his upbringing gave him a false expectation that he would survive all that life would throw at him, regardless of his crimes; because he did not, in the end, survive them – not his flight to Amsterdam as he prepared to take a ship to America and probably not his final demise, despite stories of collusion with the hangman, a protective steel collar around his neck and a doctor standing ready to revive him.

But mainly it's because he symbolised – at an extreme level – that alarming human ability to be a split personality, and as such could fairly be seen as the driving impulse behind Stevenson's still-resonant creation of Dr Jekyll and Mr Hyde.

Not convinced? You are herewith invited to read the story with sceptical eye, be carried along by it and see if, in conclusion, you disagree.

1

THE BRODIE ROOT
OF JEKYLL AND HYDE

When I was sick and lay a-bed,
I had two pillows at my head,
And all my toys beside me lay
To keep me happy all the day.

The night was a different matter. In that famous poem from his *A Child's Garden of Verses*, Robert Louis Stevenson fondly described the eponymous Land of Counterpane as 'pleasant'. But it was not always so. Sometimes, as he snuggled under his sleep-time bed-spread – or counterpane – in his second-floor room in the family house in Edinburgh's Georgian New Town, the bronchitis-affected young Robert struggled to hold back the darker side of his fertile, vivid and often fevered imagination.

It was another early affliction that he would one day turn to his own fictional advantage, but it was often scarily real at the time, exacerbated by the looming presence in his room of a tall, double-doored cabinet, which, though he once called it 'a very pretty piece of work', was pregnant with sharp meaning for him. It had been bought by his grandfather, was then owned by his father, and had an origin of unusual interest for someone who was to become a writer of spine-chilling human experience and swashbuckling adventure.

Why was it so meaningful? It had been made nearly a century before by one of Edinburgh's most notorious characters, a man whose double life still fascinates today: William Brodie. Known more commonly as Deacon Brodie – with his title as convenor of the city's Incorporation of Wrights and Masons serving almost as a forename – he sparked outrage in Edinburgh by dramatically betraying his class in having another, much darker side at play against his daytime persona, which was all about respectability. He had sartorial flair, a ready if thin-lipped smile, a family fortune, quick-witted conversation for clients and neighbours, a seat on the town council and – most impressive of all – a serious employer-career as the city's most respected cabinet-maker, who would often be expected to access his customers' shops and homes to work in situ.

It was that circumstance that helped him to become an entirely different animal by night. He was good with his hands, having acquired his skills as well as his company and fortune from his much-respected father, Francis, but it was not just woodwork that went on in his shop in the Lawnmarket (still identifiable today with the words Brodie's Close above its arched entrance). What also went on there was the repair of locks and keys, and not always for legitimate purposes. Having surreptitiously made wax or putty impressions of his clients' door keys, he then made accurate copies of them; so that after nightfall – dressed in black clothes and clutching a dark lantern – he would return to their premises as a common thief to steal their money, shop stock or valuable possessions.

Perhaps 'uncommon thief' would be a better expression, for these crimes mystified their victims, the citizens and authorities for a long time, as there was never any sign of forced entry; it looked almost as if the robber was a ghost that could pass through walls. And in the meantime, Brodie used his ill-gotten gains to maintain an extravagant lifestyle that threatened to drain his huge £10,000 legacy – an out-of-control gambling habit that included

cock-fighting, cheating with loaded dice and the expensive main-
tenance of two mistresses (who did not know of each other) with
whom he had a total of five children. But it couldn't go on forever. His first big mistake was going for a degree of delegation in
recruiting three unreliable helpers, all of whom were to eventually
betray him after his second big mistake, mounting an audacious
but abortive raid on the depository of the very taxes of Scotland –
the Excise Office at the back of Chessel's Court in the Canongate.
The handsome building can still be found there today.

What did Brodie look like? One contemporary said that, set
inside a big wig, his face looked like that of a fox, narrowing on
each side down to his chin – a good picture indeed for someone
so wily. But there was more detail. When he had been named as
the prime suspect in all these crimes, especially the tax office raid,
and the hunt was on to catch him as he took flight down through
England and across to the Continent, the following description of
him appeared in the Edinburgh press, as given in the Sheriff Clerk's
appeal for his arrest, on 12 March 1788:

WILLIAM BRODIE is about five feet four inches – is about forty-
eight years of age, but looks rather younger than he is – broad at the
shoulders and very small over the loins – has dark brown full eyes,
with large black eye-brows – under the right eye there is the scar of
a cut, which is still a little sore at the point of the eye next the nose,
and a cast with his eye that gives him somewhat the look of a Jew –
a sallow complexion – a particular motion with his mouth and lips
when he speaks, which he does full and slow, his mouth being commonly open at the time, and his tongue doubling up, as it were,
shows itself towards the roof of his mouth – black hair, twisted,
turned up, and tied behind, coming far down upon each cheek,
and the whiskers very sandy at the end; high topped in the front,
and frizzed at the side – high smooth forehead – has a particular air
in his walk, takes long steps, strikes the ground first with his heel,
bending both feet inwards before he moves them again – usually

wears a stick under hand, and moves in a proud swaggering sort of
style – his legs small above the ankle, large ankle bones and a large
foot, high brawns, small at the knees, which bend when he walks,
as if through weakness – Was dressed in a black coat, vest, breeches,
and stockings, a striped duffle great coat, and silver shoe buckles.

After he was arrested – in a rented room above a pub in Amsterdam –
and brought home to be tried and hanged, the remarkable story of
Brodie's double life and demise before 40,000 citizens, on a gibbet
often said to have been designed by himself, made him a permanently potent part of Edinburgh's lore that still held its folk in
thrall a century later. Robert Louis Stevenson was one such person,
almost obsessed not just with the literary potential of such human
duality – didn't everybody have a devil like Brodie's balancing on
one shoulder? – but by knowing that the cabinet with which he
shared his early bedroom at No. 17 Heriot Row had been designed
and made by that bad piece of work himself.

This powerful block of furniture appeared not just in his reality
but also in his dreams, even later in life; it is often claimed to have
inspired him to write at least two of his creations: first, a play entitled *Deacon Brodie or the Double Life* (co-written with his occasional
collaborator W.E. Henley) that was presented to lukewarm recep-
tions on stage in New York and London, where George Bernard
Shaw called it 'childish and unbelievable', but second, and more
importantly, his allegorical novella *Strange Case of Dr Jekyll and
Mr Hyde* that horrifically highlights the good and bad sides of a
respectable person. This not only became an instant bestseller but
also lent its title to everyday use in the English language: anyone
showing contrasting personality traits is a 'Jekyll and Hyde' character. It seemed to touch a nerve in a moment of sociological identity
crisis, while the strict mores of Victorian respectability were being
challenged by a wave of technological change.

'I want to write about a fellow who was two fellows,' the author
asserted to friends early in his career. So he spent many years

seeking an effective story to play with the idea that even good people were capable of heinous behaviour, or, as he later put it himself: 'I had long been trying to find a body, a vehicle, for that strong sense of man's double being which must at times come in upon and overwhelm the mind of every thinking creature.' There is little doubt that, for him, the Brodie theatrical creation was a big step towards 'finding' Jekyll as the holy grail.

Stevenson's stepson Lloyd Osbourne wrote:

> I don't believe that there was ever such a literary feat before as the writing of *Dr Jekyll* … Louis came downstairs in a fever; read nearly half the book aloud; and then, while we were still gasping, he was away again, and busy writing. I doubt if the first draft took so long as three days.

The good doctor's birth might have been an easier creative development than the constantly revised and reconceived Brodie play, but it was still a harsh experience. The pangs started in the author's Bournemouth health retreat in the autumn of 1885, when his American wife Fanny was alarmed at his moaning and thrashing about in bed in the small hours. She recalled: 'I was awakened by cries of horror from Louis. Thinking he had a nightmare, I awakened him. He said angrily: "Why did you wake me? I was dreaming a fine bogey tale." I had awakened him at the first transformation scene.'

He nonetheless managed to salvage many scenes from this nightmare to form the basis for the novella that has since become iconic, still a best-seller today and adapted to many feature films and countless stage plays. After it was written 'in a fever', there was more drama between the couple when he read the 'finished' story out loud to Fanny – who then suggested that he'd got it wrong, that it should have been more allegorical. He flew into another rage, threw the manuscript on the fire and ran out of the room. An hour later he was back, shouting, 'You were right, you were right!' – and immediately began scribbling again, completing a second version in another three frantic days, fuelled – some say – by drugs essentially meant for his lung condition.

What had been the problem? 'In the first draft', according to Stevenson's cousin Graham Balfour, in his *The Life of Robert Louis Stevenson* (1901), 'Jekyll's nature was bad all through and the Hyde change was worked only as a disguise.'

It was a lesson the author obviously took to heart, for in a subsequent reworking of the Brodie play he expressed his concern 'not to make Brodie pure evil'. He was certainly getting the hang of this split-personality theme that emerged again and again in his life and work. Some examples follow:

We have all our secret evil. Only mine has broken loose; it is my maniac brother who has slipped his chain.
(*Deacon Brodie* play, 1888, Act III speech)

Many a citizen was proud to welcome the Deacon to supper, and dismissed him with regret at a timeous hour, who would have been vastly disconcerted had he known how soon, and in what guise, his visitor returned.
(Robert Louis Stevenson on Deacon Brodie in *Edinburgh Picturesque Notes*)

I saw for the first time the appearance of Edward Hyde ... When I looked upon that ugly idol in the glass, I was conscious of no repugnance, rather of a leap of welcome. This, too, was myself. It seemed natural and human. In my eyes it bore a livelier image of the spirit, it seemed more express and single, than the imperfect and divided countenance I had been hitherto accustomed to call mine. And in so far I was doubtless right. I have observed that when I wore the semblance of Edward Hyde, none could come near to me at first without a visible misgiving of the flesh. This, as I take it, was because all human beings, as we meet them, are commingled out of good and evil ...

(From 'Henry Jekyll's Full Statement of the Case', chapter ten of *Strange Case of Dr Jekyll And Mr Hyde*)

It was on the moral side, and in my own person, that I learned to recognise the thorough and primitive duality of man; I saw that, of the two natures that contended in the field of my consciousness, even if I could rightly be said to be either, it was only because I was radically both.

(From the same passage as above)

But the greater question about these works that has long been open to debate is: was his haunting by the Brodie story and the Brodie bedroom cabinet the essential inspirational root for Jekyll and Hyde? It is often assumed to be the case by Robert Louis Stevenson enthusiasts, but the Edinburgh place where the six-drawer cabinet is now accommodated – in the Writers' Museum in Lady Stairs Close off the Lawnmarket, just opposite the one-time workshop of Deacon Brodie – seems to hedge its bets about that, while allowing it to be a prompter for the Brodie play. Mounted on the wall beside the exhibited curiosity, which can still send shivers running down a viewer's spine, is a caption that reads:

Cabinet of mahogany veneer, one of only two known pieces of furniture made by William Brodie (1741–1788). Deacon of the Incorporation of Wrights and a member of the Town Council of Edinburgh, Brodie led a double life by becoming a burglar by night, a crime for which he was eventually hanged.

The cabinet was in Stevenson's own room as a child, at 17 Heriot Row, and fuelled his imagination. Later, he collaborated with WE Henley in writing a play on Brodie's life, in which the cabinet was featured thus:

'And then, you know, there is the tall cabinet yonder; that it was that proved him the first of Edinburgh joiners, and worthy to be that Deacon and their head.'

(*Deacon Brodie or The Double Life*)

No mention here of Dr Jekyll, and some are not even convinced by the Brodie case. For others who can accept *some* influence, crediting the cabinet and its maker as the catalytic spark for the creation of Jekyll is definitely a step too far; they tend to reject this idea as overly convenient and romantic. But surely the best authority on what inspired the author to create Dr Jekyll would be the author himself, and here (just as the question is being addressed) comes a fortuitous development. A friend who has long been a student of Robert Louis Stevenson draws our attention to a yellowed, barely legible newspaper cutting he has just found in his garage during a house move. It contains the following words spoken by Stevenson to a *New York Herald* reporter asking him in 1887 about the genesis of Jekyll and Hyde:

EVOLVED IN DREAMS
Robert Louis Stevenson Describes How He Finds His Plots
Reporter: 'There is a great difference of opinion as to what suggested your works, particularly the *Strange Case of Dr Jekyll and Mr Hyde* and *Deacon Brodie*.'

RLS: 'Well, this has never been properly told. On one occasion I was very hard up for money and I felt that I had to do something. I thought and thought and tried hard to find a subject to write about. At night I dreamed the story, not precisely as it is written, for of course there are always stupidities in dreams, but practically it came to me as a gift, and what makes it appear more odd is that I am quite in the habit of dreaming stories. Thus, not long ago I dreamed the story of Olalla which appeared in my volume *The Merry Men*, and I have at the present moment two unwritten stories which I likewise dreamed.

'The fact is that I am so much in the habit of making stories that I go on making them while asleep quite as hard, apparently, as when I am awake. They sometimes come to me in the form of nightmares, in so far that they make me cry out loud. But I am never deceived by them. Even when fast asleep I know that it is I who am inventing and when I cry out it is with gratification to know that the story is so good. So soon as I awake, and it always awakens me when I get to a good thing, I set to work and put it together.

'For instance, all I dreamed about Jekyll was that one man was being pressed into a cabinet when he swallowed a drug and changed into another being. I awoke and said at once that I had found the missing link for which I had been looking for so long, and before I again went to sleep almost every detail of the story, as it stands, was clear to me. Of course, writing it was another thing.'

Reporter: 'Deacon Brodie?'

'I certainly didn't dream that, but in the room in which I slept as a child in Edinburgh there was a cabinet – and a very pretty piece of work it was too – from the hands of the original Deacon Brodie. When I was about nineteen years of age I wrote a sort of hugger-mugger [confused] melodrama which laid by my coffer until it was fished out by my friend WE Henley. He thought he saw something in it and we started to work together, and after a desperate campaign we turned out the original drama of Deacon Brodie as performed in London and recently, I believe, successfully in this city.

'We were both young men when we did that and I think we had an idea that bad-heartedness was strength. Now the piece has been all overhauled, and although I have no idea whether it will please an audience, I don't think either Mr Henley or I are ashamed of it. We take it now for a good, honest melodrama not so very ill done.'

So where is the magic link between Mr Brodie and Mr Hyde? His mention of 'a man being pressed into a cabinet' is a pretty clear one. But there are several other clues to the relationship in the novel.

The respectable Dr Jekyll discovers that he is able to transform himself into Mr Hyde by means of a potion and so yield to his evil side – a world of self-serving pleasure and crime that includes murder. He later writes that, as the other half of his personality, Hyde steadily became the more dominant one – ever more powerful and uncontrollable.

In his real-life experience, something similar seemed to happen to William Brodie as he became – despite having some redeeming traits such as love for his families, some erudition, a sense of humour and a superficially charming way with people – totally possessed by his wicked other side.

The similarities between him and Stevenson's fictional bad guy are often noticeable in the novel. At one point, for instance, Mr Utterson, the lawyer, comments: 'This Master Hyde, if he were studied … must have secrets of his own; black secrets by the look of him; secrets compared to which poor Jekyll's worst would be like sunshine … it turns me cold to think of this creature stealing like a thief.'

In his 1955 book *The Fabulous Originals*, Irving Wallace points out what he believes are more borrowings from Brodie's life, such as: Hyde was once discovered in his laboratory disguised by a mask and Brodie often employed crepe masks in his double life; after the murder, Hyde had a song upon his lips as he compounded the draught, and Brodie had a song upon his lips on the eve of his greatest crime; Hyde dressed himself in black, as Brodie did – shedding his daytime white jacket and breeches – when morphing into his bad self and heading out on a robbery; Brodie used various houses, just as Jekyll and Hyde lived in various houses.

And where were the houses? There has long been a question mark over the Jekyll setting. It is supposed to be London, but Scots readers in particular tend to recognise that 'the black old streets in which Hyde slinks on his evil path amidst carefully undescribed squalor and committing, for the most part, carefully unspecified sins, are Edinburgh streets'. So asserted author Moray McLaren in his 1950 centenary book *Stevenson and Edinburgh*, adding:

The heavily furnished, lamp-shaded interior of Dr Jekyll's unostentatiously prosperous house is the inside of any well-to-do professional man's home in the New Town of Edinburgh. The contrast is not so much between black evil and golden goodness as between dark dirt and gloomy respectability. The stage throughout is only half lit. It is an Edinburgh Winter's Night tale.

★★★

That prosperous New Town house was familiar enough to Stevenson, as it was in such a home that he lived from the age of six to his university years. Today, the elegantly Georgian No. 17 Heriot Row, built in 1804, remains very much as he left it – minus the furniture he had taken to Samoa on moving there for his health in 1890 – and the current owners, John and Felicitas Macfie, are devoted not just to the building's continuing welfare but to the idea that genuinely interested people can share it to some extent. While stressing that it is a private home and not a museum, they are relaxed about opening it up to bed-and-breakfast guests and special-occasion parties, and they kindly gave this writer a tour that included the very bedroom where Robert Louis Stevenson had those very dreams in full view of that very 'inspirational' cabinet.

It is a modest room, about 10ft by 20ft, with one square, cross-hatched window facing out on to the street. It is easy to picture the 'two pillows at my head' by that window and take in his view back into the room, where that cabinet – to the right of the door as he looked ahead – would have stood directly in front of him with a gap between it and the bed.

It is easy to imagine, too, how it would have occupied and dominated his waking moments as well as his dreams; how its big, brown bear-like silhouette might have ignited nightmares – which in turn would have prompted his flight to nursemaid Allison Cunningham (Cummy, as he knew her) in her back room with a view over to Fife, just a few steps along the adjoining corridor. That's where she, and often his father Thomas – famed builder of remote Scottish lighthouses – would show their softer side, comforting the troubled boy and telling him romantic stories that would fire his fertile imagination in, we assume, a different way from the bad dreams.

Indeed, there was much comfort and beauty there for him – not least in the drawing room with its Victorian furnishing, grand piano and three tall windows looking out over the site of that famous gas lamp, whose human lighter inspired him to write the words:

For we are very lucky, with a lamp before the door,
And Leerie stops to light it as he lights so many more;
And O! before you hurry by with ladder and with light,
O Leerie, see a little child and nod to him tonight!

It was here, in this room, that his literary talent was first recognised – by one of his mother's friends. His mother, Margaret, 'had been ridiculing him in the way that mothers of teenage boys do, in their exasperation,' says John Macfie, 'when Robert appeared – having overheard it – and protested: "I'm not as bad as you're painting me!" He was then persuaded to read out one of his poems to his mother's friend, the wife of a London university professor, who was visiting, and she was so impressed that she introduced RLS and his work to various London literary circles. That was the start of his becoming known outside his home.'

And he sensed there was much more to be experienced beyond that front-door lamp. Gradually, he grew away from the ever-so-Presbyterian Cummy and, when he got off to university, 'he felt then free to keep bad company'. How bad was it? 'Pretty bad,' says Macfie, a lawyer in his day job, with six children ranging from 22 to 7 years old. 'He relished the dark and the light; loved picturing himself – this rebellious teenager – sitting in a brothel parlour by the stove, with long hair and a red velvet jacket, writing bad poetry and being mothered by the girls.'

The source of this revelation? The man himself. He admitted in his letters that he kept 'very mixed company' that would be regularly renewed by the actions of the police and magistrates. It got to the stage that, addressing a friend, he volubly appreciated his elegant home not for its beauty or comfort but for the fact that its stairs up to his bedroom were made of stone rather than wood; so that when he came home in the dead of night, there would be no creaking to be heard.

When Stevenson escaped from his *douce* middle-class life into the murky, sexy Old Town underworld, it was, of course, that split-personality syndrome rising to the surface as it would repeatedly for the rest of his life – and as it surely did, even more dramatically, with Deacon Brodie. 'I think what RLS was going through was similar to that which had gripped Brodie,' says John Macfie. 'It was the adrenalin rush of being bad – of maybe being caught, maybe not. It was exciting for him – for them – to get ever-nearer to the edge.'

Indeed, he almost saw the other side of that coin as sinful in its own way. The sins he attributed to Jekyll were the essential Edinburgh ones of secrecy and puritanism that governed his youth, and – like many other socially inhibited people of that time and place – the author was tempted every so often to reject it. His consequent bad behaviour is quite widely acknowledged by writers and students of his life and work. Examples? The Edinburgh crime writer Ian Rankin wrote, 'As a teenager, he would tiptoe from the family home at dead of night and make his way to the more anarchic and seamy Old Town where drunks cavorted with harlots and a man could let his hair down.' This is echoed by the Boston College 'horror professor' Raymond McNally, who said RLS defied 'the staid British Victorian traits of propriety and piety by engaging in his own secret life of narcotics, alcohol and sexual decadence', adding: 'He was overtly respectable but loved to frequent – in his words – the whores and thieves in the lower part of town.'

His wanderings into the dark side were not like Hyde's joyless lust for evil, however; they were powered by bohemian romanticism verging on fantasy. And the ghost of Deacon Brodie would have been ever-present here for him too, walking at his shoulder in smirking silence, risen from the living man's recall of long Old Town walks with Cummy in his childhood 'where he could still see the narrow, alley-like sidestreet that was Brodie's Close, and the court and mansion, with its elaborate oaken door, where Brodie and his sister had entertained Scottish gentry'.

Here society's contrasts were tightly focused – especially before the advent of the population-splitting New Town in the mid-eighteenth century – where rich and poor, good and evil had long lived alongside each other around that narrow ridge of rock on which most of the city's history had been played out. The human capacity for these differences to be contained within individual hypocritical personalities simply fascinated Robert Louis Stevenson. In his mind they were all dramatically personified in Brodie, who strutted these streets by day – with a fancy walking stick for effect – and lurked within its shadowy closes by night, clutching a dark lantern under a black cloak.

The closes were the narrow alleys that separated the towering buildings known in these days as 'lands', where some floors were so unreachably sky-high – up to twelve levels – that older folk became marooned, with only more youthful, helpful others to depend on for provisions of water, food and coal. 'It was at one point the worst housing in Europe,' comments John Macfie.

★★★

But do we have a straight lineage from Brodie to Jekyll/Hyde? A particular strand tends to be drawn on – often by zealous student observers – to claim the idea of a direct literary inspiration. But surely most writers themselves will shy from crediting this or that spark as an immediate prompting for any idea, believing more in an amalgam of influences. In the case of Stevenson's *Treasure Island*, for instance, a variety of prompters are put forward for the island model: a map he spontaneously drew to entertain his stepson Lloyd in the late Miss MacGregor's cottage in Braemar, 'with the rain hammering against the window'; his regular views of the seabird-whitened islet of Fidra off the shore of North Berwick;

and those of another muddy, nameless islet he knew in the fast-flowing Allanwater near the cave that 'inspired' his home for Ben Gunn. Talking of which, in the actual town of Bridge of Allan where he spent many a family holiday, there was (and still is) a chemist's shop he frequented, where the hunched apothecary is said to have given him a model for Hyde.

And in the same way, all kinds of other factors from the author's experience have crowded into the scenario of Jekyll (pronounced in Scots like 'treacle'). There were his 'Brownies' – the little people who visited his dreams with their own ideas worth developing; there was the influence of family friend James Simpson, whose story of conducting the first trial of chloroform in 1847 surely influenced his thinking about powerful personality-changing potions; and, yes, there was Brodie.

He has sometimes been called 'the father' of Jekyll and Hyde, and a few scholars have taken issue with that, just as they might with the title of this book – *The Man Who Was Jekyll and Hyde* – arguing that he was, of course, a different person (or persons, if you like); but it can't be denied that William Brodie was, as literary influences go, quite exceptional; in a class of his own. It seems justifiable then, without even trying to claim him as direct inspiration, that this concept can be comfortably embraced with a mere smidgen of poetic licence.

So let's say it: the lineage, or building blocks, of the Jekyll tale came in large degree from the real-life double-life man, through the Brodie bedroom cabinet and stage-play, and out through the dream-with-cabinet into the creation of the split-personality doctor.

But this book is not all about that. It is the remarkable story of the human enigma that was Deacon Brodie himself. The man who defied his class and his own societal grooming to become a rampant robber of his own friends and business contacts. Was he just weak? Just evil? Just romantic? Just mischievous? Keen to be contrary just for the sake of it? Or all of these things and more?

Whatever he was – as Stevenson discovered and believed for most of his life – he was a man of many mysterious dimensions.

The following pages tell his tale without further comment, inviting the reader to reach his or her own conclusions about the Strange Case of Deacon William Brodie.

2

HIS LIFE AND LOVES

The yellow leaflet that sits on every table beside the menu says most of it, really. The off-street café that today occupies Brodie's Close, the cavernous Lawnmarket premises where the Brodie family once lived and worked, is called, aptly enough, The Deacon's House Café. It serves up lots of facts about our anti-hero – printed beside his etched image on that leaflet – along with its range of 'home-made soups, freshly prepared salads and sandwiches with an excellent selection of home baking and puddings'.

The close, or alleyway, was originally named after Francis, the family's pillar of the community back then. But it is his infamous son we think of when visiting it now. Beside its potted biography of Brodie junior – a full-colour, full-size effigy of whom stands guard at the close-mouth pavement – the busy tourist-attracting establishment tells its own part in his tale:

The present café was at one time Deacon Brodie's workshop. The Brodie house, which no longer exists, was probably further down the close which at one time extended all the way down to Cowgate. When the property was renovated in 1962 the remnants of swords, muskets and uniforms were discovered under the floorboards of the café. These may have been hidden there by soldiers during the uprising in 1745. The stone archway in the kitchen area dates back to 1420, when monks used the cellar as a brewing house.

Indeed, as we sit at one of about sixteen tables, enjoying its fine coffee and shortbread, that original stonework is still to be seen behind the servers' display cabinet where the relatively new French owner Philippe Bachelet is also to be found. It somehow adds to the frisson of realisation that we are in the presence of history, in the very place not just where medieval Cambusnethan monks baked and brewed for charity but where Deacon Brodie's eighteenth-century furniture was created. Reminders of that, in the form of newspaper cuttings featuring the notorious one-time proprietor, are pinned around the nearby wood-slatted wall, while the close-side wall with its three main windows sees the start of Andrew Glen's room-circling biographical mural that illustrates the Deacon's tale from 1745 to 1788, ending with how his misadventures inspired Robert Louis Stevenson to create the double character of Jekyll and Hyde. Its timeline goes like this, starting with a panel that recalls:

1745: Bonnie Prince Charlie with the Jacobite army and his arrival at Edinburgh, when William Brodie would have been four years old.

1782: Young Brodie acquires the family cabinet-making firm on his father's death.

1785: Cabinet-makers at work in Brodie's workshop, now the seating area of the café.

1786: Robert Burns visits Edinburgh and lives briefly in a house directly opposite Brodie's Close.

1787: Brodie in the act of robbing a neighbour.

1788: The game is up! Brodie is arrested in Amsterdam.

1788: 1st October. Brodie and his accomplice George Smith are hanged.

1876: Robert Louis Stevenson writes a play called *Deacon Brodie or the Double Life*. This is followed ten years later by *Jekyll and Hyde*.

The upper part of the building is now used by its masonic owners, the Celtic Lodge Edinburgh and Leith No. 291, and it's there that a visitor can get up close and personal with more spine-tingling links to the Brodies, father and son. In the temple at the top, where serious masonic business takes place, there is a mural showing the Brodies' creation of 'a marble table supported by an eagle burnished with gold' and supplied to the Duke of Gordon; this accounted for the Roman Eagle Hall name of the biggest room – the size of a small church hall – where lodge members enjoy regular social 'harmony' gatherings. Once used as an extra workshop-cum-showroom for the Brodies' products, it is now called the Thistle Room and is remarkable for what some suggest is the spiritual 'possession' of a large, ornately framed mirror near its entrance.

'Because of it our cleaning lady will not go near the Thistle Room or Temple on her own,' says Bill Boland, the lodge's past master, treasurer and historian. Why? 'One night, not twenty years ago, another past master was locking up securely for the night when, on glancing at the mirror, he noticed a shadowy figure appearing within it – and he swore it was Deacon Brodie, dressed in his finest, with three-pointed hat and formal tails.'

Any other eerie moments? 'Nothing specific,' he says, 'but we have been visited over the years by quite a few psychics and they all say there is a very cold aura emanating from the mirror – which I don't think was made by Brodie, who was himself a freemason with Canongate-Kilwinning Lodge No. 2. They say it suggests the presence of someone; and indeed one claimed what they had perceived was the spirit of Bonnie Prince Charlie.'

When you consider this characterful building and its imaginative café alongside the impressively high-profile pub named after Brodie just across the cobbled Lawnmarket street – with its highly graphic 'good' and 'bad' Brodie hanging signs – you can't escape the thought that if the unlikely outlaw's outlandish activities didn't do much for his city's reputation at the time, they left it with quite a romantic folk-tale legacy which it is quite happy to exploit these days.

But while these colourful establishments fit, in one way, with the general circus that is Edinburgh's Old Town in the tourist-invaded summer – the ranks of shops selling rain-creased tartan tat as a backdrop to Festival-drawn thespians whose impromptu open-air performances magnetise crowds along the Royal Mile – they are also rather different, sincerely acknowledging in their own way a slice of Edinburgh's rich history, albeit a less-than-honourable one. It has to be added that there are many fine shops here too, selling cashmere and whisky and international newspapers and fine food. It all adds up to a kaleidoscopic assault on the senses.

But it was not always so dazzlingly bright around here. The colours in those far-off eighteenth-century days, when the relatively dashing Deacon Brodie walked these cobbles in all his apparent respectability, were much more muted. Especially after darkness fell and the myriad closes between the sky-high tenements or 'lands' in all four sections of what is now known as the Royal Mile, running from the castle down to the Palace of Holyroodhouse – Castlehill, the Lawnmarket, the High Street and the Canongate – became shadowy refuges for those who would do you harm, little worried about relieving you of your money or your valuables or your life. A point with which our Mr Brodie was perhaps just a little too familiar.

The gutters ran 'as big as burns', reported a resident of the time. And if you wandered off the beaten track after a night at the club or tavern, it was spooky and dangerous, dark and overpoweringly smelly. This thanks not only to the elevated residents slopping out their human waste to the walkways below at the day's end – while famously crying out 'Gardyloo!' to alert passers-by – but also to horses and the proximity of the Nor' Loch which, before becoming the fragrant Princes Street Gardens, was a stagnant cesspool for the submergence of every unpleasantness imaginable, including bodies and parts thereof.

Oh, and of course, there were the fish.

The fish? Not the kind that might have lived (or more likely, died) in a filthy pond like that, but fish from the cleaner waters around Newhaven and Leith that were buyable at the Fishmarket Close or from wandering, basket-laden fishwives. These fish, after being relieved of much flesh, would be used for a certain degree of illumination along these dreadfully dingy closes. Their scales would be luminescent enough to justify wary residents nailing the skins at intervals along the closes' lowering walls. They did not exactly light up the scene like sunshine but certainly, on ageing, could pick out a direction of travel, rather like the emergency floor lights in modern aircraft, while adding to the general odour.

It was understandable that people craved to see where they were going as they made their way through the overcrowded Old Town, down these dark narrow alleys and up the exhaustingly steep climb to their cold, cramped homes – which could be as high as twelve storeys before touching the clouds. In the absence of gas or electric street lighting and given the outdoor uselessness of unprotected beeswax or tallow candles, there were only one or two other ways of easing your nocturnal fears and discomforts. It did not give out much light, but the whale-oil-fired street lamp, occasionally protruding from its street wall mounting, was a lot better than nothing. Then there was the hand-carried dark lantern as favoured by Deacon Brodie on his night-time adventures, the 'dark' meaning that its candle-flame could be closed off to the elements (and indoor curious eyes) by means of a sliding shutter. And there were the young lads – or 'caddies' – with burning-brand torches who would see people safely home for a price.

Once indoors, the piscatorial pong would be even stronger, as fish sustained the people – packed like sardines themselves – not only as food but also as a source of oil for their 'cruisie' lamps. Fuel was also needed for warmth, cooking and the boiling of water, and all of these heavy essentials had to find their way up the steep and filthy, urine-smelling common stairs. Enter again, the blue-bonneted caddies, some of whom would specialise in carrying water barrels on their backs.

Caddies? Readers will be familiar with the word as used to describe a golfer's club-carrier, and while its provenance is not entirely clear, owing something to the French word *cadet* – for a military officer's helper – it seems to have reached the International Open courses via a circuitous route from the capital of the cradle of golf, where it depicted something akin to a street messenger. Described by the chronicler Robert Chambers as 'ragged and half-blackguard-looking', caddies were nonetheless allowed to be 'amazingly acute and intelligent' … and, apparently, trustworthy.

They were mainly rough-and-ready characters from the Highlands who – always for a price – would employ their raw power to perform the carrying feats that kept the tenement dwellers alive. But that was only part of their repertoire. They were also guides, gossip-mongers, people-finders and general dogsbodies (an interesting word in view of the fact that in the mid-1700s they were employed by the town council to catch and kill every dog they saw to prevent the spread of rabies). Edinburgh's first historian, William Maitland, described them as 'errand-men, news-cryers or pamphlet-sellers' who, as of 1714, became an organised society subject to regulation and supervision by the council, responsible for upholding the monopoly of members' activities in the city. Council magistrates determined the number of members, who each wore a standard-issue blue linen apron as a badge of identification 'which none may lend on pain of losing his privilege'.

Congregating around the central Mercat Cross near St Giles cathedral and summoned with the call 'caddie!' on a first come, first served basis, they had strict rules of behaviour in each other's interest, with Rule 5 saying: 'When one is called to go an errand, or sell a paper, where two or more are present, he who cometh first to the person who called him, shall have the benefit of what is sold or had for going the errand, unless the person who called otherwise determine it.'

You couldn't be in the city for more than a few hours, wrote the young visiting Englishman Edward Topham in his *Letters from Edinburgh* in the mid-1770s …

... Before being watched, and your name, and place of abode, found out by the Cadies ... and they are of great utility, as without them it would be very difficult to find anybody, on account of the great height of the houses, and the number of families in every building. [They] faithfully execute all commands at a very reasonable price. Whether you are in need of a *valet de place*, a pimp, a thief-catcher, or a bully, your best resource is to the fraternity of Cadies. In short, they are the tutelary guardians of the City, and it is entirely owing to them, that there are fewer robberies, and less house-breaking in Edinburgh, than any where else.

Another Englishman – an army officer – recalled in the 1750s how he was guided to his lodgings at night, just as the beat of the city drum signalled the time for residents to empty their chamber-pots from their windows with that cry of 'Gardyloo!' (from the French *gardez vous de l'eau:* watch out for the water). 'The guide went before me to prevent my disgrace, crying out all the way, with a loud voice, "Hud your haunds". The throwing up of a sash, or otherwise opening a window, made me tremble, while behind and before me, at some little distance, fell the terrible shower.'

With water being newly piped to houses instead of being drawn from communal street-wells, the caddies and their *raison d'être* within the city disappeared in the early part of the next century – but not before being taken up by the embryonic golfing fraternity, the gentlemen of Edinburgh who hired them to carry their golf clubs when playing on Leith Links and Bruntsfield Links.

Anyway, the growing favour being won by this civilised sport among wealthier sections in Brodie's time – when George III benignly ruled the joined-up post-Culloden British nations while the American colonies were going their independent way and the French were about to revolt against their aristocracy – indicated that there was another side to the chaotic, unruly and often belligerent life of what could be truly a hell of a city.

And yet, and yet ...

Visiting travellers, like the 24-year-old Topham, had often gasped at its theatrical elegance, despite the rough human texture that lay beneath, and in a period of relative stability and generally buried differences with the outside world, its other, shinier side began to push ahead in the reputational stakes.

While this Other Edinburgh was growing into a dramatic stage for intellectual enlightenment, attracting some of the country's best brains, the city's physical beauty was also being enhanced with many expensive new public buildings created in the Greek neo-classical style, so that it would sometimes be known as the 'Athens of the North'. And to top it all there was the New Town, a monumental new architectural endeavour which, despite still having rather basic lavatories, was to organise the city on an elegant grid system and tempt the professional classes from the Old Town over to the previously underdeveloped north of the city, where their successors are still to be found today.

Not that the more refined citizenry had been getting their footwear dirty on the slimy, slippery cobbled surfaces of the High Street. Fine ladies in long dresses over many petticoats could lift themselves above the mucky surface by fixing iron pattens to their shoes. For others who would normally travel by carriage – but couldn't here because of the tight thoroughfare and narrow closes between the tall houses – there was always the sedan chair. Perhaps that should be plural, chairs, as there were two types: those ornately decorated models owned by the well-heeled and the less fancy black-painted utilitarian types of the time, which were for hire in the manner of today's black cabs.

What did it cost? The sedan tariff list of around 1770 – when a pair of chickens cost 1s (one shilling, about 5p today) and home rentals between £1 and £20 a year depending on social status – gives the price of a whole day's hire as 4s (20p), while a single journey within the city would be 6d (2.5p). It was at least another shilling on top of that for any journey half a mile beyond the city limits.

The contraption, in which passengers could travel from door to door and even from one building's interior to another, was carried by two muscular men, usually Highlanders again, with one trudging on ahead and one skittering along behind. And the gentleman or lady so keen to avoid the filthy streets touching their expensive clothes would enter from the front so that the carrying bars would not have to be removed.

It was, after all, a tough enough job for the carriers, as many of their customers were heavy and drunkenly relaxed old men. His brawny helpers also had to be rain and cold resistant, as sedan chairs were much in demand in bad weather — just like today's taxis.

There were no such weighty challenges with the lighter package of Mr Brodie, though he was quite capable of being tipsy. Sometimes, of course, the sedan would take him to places that might suggest this apparently respectable businessman, councillor and Deacon of Wrights, this pillar of society was rather cracked and leaning — or at the very least a little off-centre. So how did he escape public censure for so long? How did he engender such discretion in such men if not through the look-what-we-have-in-common touch? And there were more surprisingly shrugged shoulders. Apart from all their other duties, the town centre's army of caddies heard and saw everything of any interest in and around their patch. As such, they were the eyes and ears of the Town Guard, another colourful body of men, who, as the forerunners of the police when law enforcement was left entirely to local initiative, should have at least been interested in Mr Brodie's already suspect nocturnal doings.

Colourful? Well, to a degree. Dressed in faded red uniforms and plumed hats, the Town Guard consisted of about 120 men officially devoted to guardianship of the city and preservation of public order. They were present on all public occasions but only a limited number were regularly on duty. The rest were allowed to work at their trades, subject to being called out at a moment's notice. In truth, the body was something of a Dad's Army, composed mainly of discharged soldiers who were still able – just – to shoulder a musket or wield a Lochaber axe and use them in a street brawl.

The young poet Robert Fergusson, who died four years before Brodie's demise, called them 'that black banditti', having encountered their tender mercies too often after his 'regular bacchanalian irregularities'. Sir Walter Scott wrote of them that, being generally Highlanders:

> They were, neither by birth, education, nor former habits, trained to endure with much patience the insults of the rabble; or the provoking petulance of truant-boys, and idle debauchees, of all descriptions, with whom their occupation brought them into contact. On the contrary, the tempers of the poor old fellows were soured by the indignities with which the mob distinguished them … On all occasions – when holiday licensed some riot or irregularity – a skirmish with these veterans was a favourite recreation with the rabble of Edinburgh.

Nevertheless, it remains a mystery how Brodie's capricious ways and 'protracted peccadilloes' (Roughhead's words) somehow escaped the attentions of the Guardsmen even at the very beginning of his criminal career. It was to become highly suspected at one point that he had helped spring a convicted and condemned criminal from the Tolbooth Prison and had him hidden, fed and watered within the grandiose Greyfriars tomb of Sir George Mackenzie, tormentor of the Covenanters a century before. But nothing could actually be pinned on him. And indeed, until the very end, Brodie retained the respect and esteem of his fellow citizens, as he went about his daily business, regularly attending council meetings, and latterly even sharing his colleagues' anguish at the dreadful series of crimes that had befallen the great old capital. Even more puzzling with hindsight was the apparent lack of neighbour-to-neighbour gossip about him, when 'stairhead' scandal was a phenomenon well recognised by Fergusson:

Now Stairhead Critics, senseless Fools,
Censure their Aim, and Pride their Rules,
In Luckenbooths, wi' glouring Eye,
Their Neighbours sma'est Faults descry:
If ony Loun should dander there,
Of aukward Gate, and foreign Air,
They trace his Steps, till they can tell
His Pedigree as weel's himsell.

Luckenbooths? Built around 1460, these 'locked booths' housed Edinburgh's first permanent shops, sitting in a row of seven tenement buildings connected to the Old Tolbooth Prison and running parallel to St Giles Cathedral. Originally exclusive to goldsmiths and jewellers, they later housed 'ane chymist and druggist', a baker, milliner, hairdresser and even a toyshop.

★★★

With the great looming bulks of St Giles and the Tolbooth centrally dominating all proceedings, and the potential targets of many more side-by-side shops lining the route between the closes, this then was the condensed world of William Brodie. His life, his work, his home, his leisure and his loves – not to mention his crimes – were all concentrated around this mile-long encapsulation of human life and all its failings and foibles. The many layers of its deeply textured society provided an aptly confusing backdrop for the identity crisis from which he obviously suffered. For while he would often avail himself of a sedan chair as a member of the city elite, he also felt something acutely in common with the simple men who carried him there. The feeling was almost mutual, as the customer who was described in some accounts as 'small and slender' was easier to carry than most, as well as quite affable and able to show the common touch. But it wasn't as simple as that, of course.

He clearly enjoyed his gentleman status too. Obviously well educated – not far from home in James Mundell's exclusive 'humanities' school in West Bow – and a man of considerable wit and charm as well as political influence, property and monetary wealth, with £10,000 (worth £850,000 today) left by his father he should have had no need to dabble in a life of crime and mix with 'the lower orders'. But he clearly had a fancy to, and a simple need did eventually arise – a serious shortfall in income brought about by his big gambling losses and the costs of keeping two families – which played right into his psyche of considerable complexity. How? The clue was perhaps his love of theatre and the theatrical. In all his 'below-the-line' dealings, one major motive force seemed to be romance. Or drama. Or infamy. Or something that made him out of the ordinary, adventurous, even piratical. If he hadn't needed money, lion-taming might have been up his street.

This need for an exciting frisson of danger also ran through his recreation, business and love life. His enthusiasm for opera, which saw (or heard) him constantly singing operatic songs at work that irritated his colleagues and sisters, was perhaps the mildest of his passions. If we ignore for a moment the early signs of his crossing the crime line, there was the club life, the cards, the cockfights, the above-mentioned mistresses and their dependent families by him, all of which were expensive. This man of means gave a sharper meaning to the phrase 'disposable income': he simply did not seem capable of holding on to his, despite that impressive inheritance, his successful business and his ownership of considerable property other than the family complex in Brodie's Close. There were at least three other tenements in his name, at the Nether Bow and in World's End Close. Council records also show that in 1785, two years before he turned to crime in desperation, he was speculating in the building lots of the New Town (see chapter 3). And in 1789, after the game was up and he had swung for it, there was a house in Old Bank Close that was purchased from the trustee for his creditors by William Martin, bookseller and auctioneer in Edinburgh, who then sold it to the Bank of Scotland four years later.

He could have used all that silver-spoon wealth in a slower enjoyment of the good life, but when it came to nightlife, he was attracted to the bad life like a moth to a candle, and in the same way managed to burn his own wings and destroy himself. Almost inevitably, he was a slave to, and perhaps even a victim of ...

The Club Life

There was no shortage of taverns and drinking dens in the city where, after work, the social classes mixed a bit more freely than at work. Only fallen women allowed, of course. But for those gentlemen who could afford it there were the tucked-away clubs – with all kinds of unusual names and themes which were mostly, to put it politely, rather naughty. Bawdy songs – some even penned by Robert Burns – were a specialty of the Crochallan. The Dirty Club was not entirely subtle about its interests, and there were others with strange names and rituals: the Poker, the black Wigs, the Spendthrift, the Odd Fellows – where members wrote their names upside-down. Many businessmen were also members of Freemasonry lodges whose rituals were even more esoteric.

But it was the Cape Club to which the thrill-hungry William Brodie was most attracted. This most famous of the city's social clubs held its meetings in James Mann's tavern, also known as The Isle of Man Arms, in Craig's Close. He liked this club not just because he needed to eat of an evening but also because he was disinclined to break off his convivialities to go home and do so – wherever home might be that night: his own house or either one of his mistresses'. And he liked it not just because of its culinary offerings but because of its central theme of (often sexual) fantasy. Ostensibly a supper club serving meals – such as Welsh rarebit and Loch Fyne herring and London porter – the Cape had many depths and dimensions that clearly intrigued Brodie. There were good (or bad) reasons why it magnetised him: the genuinely artistic and merchants and manufacturers who claimed appreciation of the Arts. Apart from the glovers, bakers, fish-hook makers, lawyers, tanners, surgeons and insurance brokers, it drew touring thespians from the Theatre Royal and some of Scotland's most celebrated artistic names. Notably on the roll of the Knights Companions of the Cape were the painters John Bonnar, Alexander Runciman and Henry Raeburn, the writer David Herd and Robert Fergusson – who met his premature and untimely death four months before William Brodie was elected to the club in February 1775.

So what was so exotic about it? Each new member was required, while suggestively holding a poker with his left hand that might then fall to rest on his crotch, to solemnly speak the oath before the president in a red velvet cap:

> I swear devoutly by this light
> To be a true and faithful Knight
> With all my might, both day and night
> So help me Poker!

The new member then had to assume some fanciful personal title carrying rude innuendo with allusions to his character or misadventures. There was a Sir Stark Naked and a Sir Roger; Mr Raeburn was Sir Discovery long before he was actually knighted by the king, while Mr Fergusson was Sir Precentor, who caught the spirit of the club in his verse and self-sung song. Brodie took the title of Sir Lluyd, and tales were by all, amid loud hilarity, of sexual adventures and conquests.

But his fellow members did not remain faithful to him to the end. After his last public appearance on the scaffold thirteen years later, the grim scene was recorded by the sketch of a mischievous colleague on the margin of the roll prefixed to the club's minute-book.

As William Roughead wrote in his book *Trial of Deacon Brodie* of 1906, 'Had the young Brodie been satisfied with the legitimate and very ample convivialities afforded by the Cape Club it would have been better for himself. But …'

The Cards

'Brodie became a frequenter of a rough tavern kept by the vintner James Clark, at the head of the Fleshmarket Close, where gambling by dice was practised nightly among a band of disreputable twitchers and crook-fingered Jacks.'

He had doubtless cheated here before, but one night's work came back to haunt him after a worse-for-wear James Hamilton, the master of the city's chimney sweeps, edged his way into the Brodie party, who (they said later) had been 'innocently amusing themselves with a game of dice over a glass of punch'.

The master sweep was ushered into the amusement – 'suspecting no fraud or deceit' – but within a few minutes found himself relieved of 'five guinea notes, two half guineas in gold, and six shillings in silver'. So outraged was he that he seized the dice, found them to be loaded – filled with lead at one corner – and, after an altercation that resulted in Brodie thereafter bearing an ugly scar around one eye, decided to take the case to higher authority. He petitioned the town council demanding that the Deacon of Wrights and his gang be arrested and made to pay damages.

Brodie defended himself with the reply that 'if false dice were used on that occasion, it was unknown to the defenders as the dice they played with belonged to the house'. And he concluded that 'the petitioner is a noted adept in the science of gambling, and it was not very credible that he would have allowed himself to be imposed upon in the manner he had alleged'.

Hamilton's sarcastic response was biting:

Mr Brodie knows nothing of such vile tricks – not he! He never made them his study – not he! Mr Brodie never haunted night houses, where nothing but the blackest and vilest arts were practised to catch a pigeon! He never was accessory, either by himself or others in his combination, to behold the poor young creature plucked alive, and not one feather left upon its wings – not he, indeed! He never was accessory to see or be concerned in fleecing the ignorant, the thoughtless, the young, and the unwary, nor ever made it his study, his anxious study, with unwearied concern, at midnight hours, to haunt the rooms where he thought of meeting with the company from which there was a possibility of fetching from a scurvy sixpence to a hundred guineas – not he, indeed! He is unacquainted altogether either with packing or shuffling a set of cards – he is, indeed!

It was some kind of a comment on the moral standards of the time that the council stood by its own, even one of whom there were growing doubts, and – perhaps well pierced by such keen comments – nevertheless decided to take the matter no further.

The Cockfights

Flying feathers and blood amid the squawking of distressed birds fighting to the death, added to the bawling of excited male spectators, doesn't sound much like a sport for noble souls. But cockfighting in Brodie's time was called a 'gentlemanly vice' – as a fashionable recreation among the capital's young bloods – and he developed such a passion for it that he even bred and maintained his own game cocks in a pen in his wood-yard.

It was not just the cock-fighting blood as such that excited him, of course, as a regular attender at the 'mains' held in the cockpit belonging to his friend Michael Henderson, stabler in the Grassmarket. He is said to have loved betting on the sport – and he was not always a winner, of course.

He was present, among other 'eminent cockers' at the historic match between the counties of Lanark and Haddington, of which an account is given in *Kay's Edinburgh Portraits*, published in 1885: 'This affair was decided in the unfinished kitchen of the Assembly Rooms, in 1785; on which occasion the gentlemen cockfighters of the county of East Lothian were the victors. Among the audience will be recognised likenesses of the principal individuals of this fancy at the time.' He particularly points out Sir James Baird of Newbyth, William Hamilton of Wishaw (later Lord Belhaven) and 'the noted Deacon Brodie, and several other eminent cockers'.

Kay also commented: 'It cannot but appear surprising that noblemen and gentlemen, who upon any other occasion will hardly show the smallest degree of condescension to their inferiors, will, in the prosecution of this barbarous amusement, demean themselves so far as to associate with the very lowest characters in society.'

That kind of self-demeaning was another sport that Deacon Brodie was not averse to, enjoying as he did the company of low characters; so 'the art of cocking' was right up his street and he maintained his enthusiasm for it until the day he died, even writing to ask for updates on results while he was on the run abroad.

However, there is no doubt that it caused him to lose a small fortune and little doubt that his nocturnal adventures helped supplement his investments in it. One suspects he might not have worried about a little cheating here and there too ... as with the cards.

The Mistresses

Brodie was not just a cheat at cards. He was obviously unfaithful to his mistresses, at least with regard to each other. Until the very public last moments of his life, they apparently knew nothing of each other. While officially, and before the eyes of the general public, he had lived respectably with his housekeeper-sister Jean in their house at the foot of the Lawnmarket close, the Deacon's 'over-relaxed' evenings often ended in either of two other beds – one in Cant's Close belonging to Anne Grant, with whom he had a family of three children, and one in the nearby house of Jean Watt, whose two boys he had fathered, though in one of his frequent poisonous spats with her he had expressed some doubt about the paternity of one of them.

Nonetheless, possibly for no other reason than the close proximity of Miss Watt's home – in the no-longer-extant Libberton's Wynd, only a few score yards from his – he would often make an impulsive diversion in the moonlight and wake up in the sunlight of her bed of a morning.

Such bedtimes often happened after his criminal forays, and it seems that, while generally being tolerant and welcoming of his unannounced arrivals, she did not ask too many questions. To recount Forbes Bramble's imagined scenario of one such evening, just after Brodie tried to rob a tobacconist's shop:

> 'Are ye sober?'
>
> 'Of course I'm sober!'
>
> 'Well, will ye tak off your clothes and cam tae bed, or am I tae wait a' nicht! And me needin' ma sleep!'
>
> She turned back the bedclothes invitingly. Jean Watt was dark-haired, dark-eyed and attractive. She wordlessly gathered her linen nightdress by the hem and pulled it up to her chin. Will, swearing to himself, tore off his cloak and shoes and scrambled down over her.
>
> 'Tak your time, Will Brodie! Dinna wouf a guid thing! Ye smell terrible o' tabacca!'
>
> 'You're a devil, Jean, you're a devil!'
>
> Jean smiled contentedly and knowingly over his shoulder, Men were such excellent plain fools.

It happened again (or did it?) after his fateful attempt to raid the Excise Office, the crime on which his trial focused. Jean Watt stepped forward as a witness in a bid to give him an alibi and told the court (see chapter 6) that she was well acquainted with the prisoner, 'having a family of children to him', and added:

I remember that on Wednesday the 5th of March last [the night of the raid] Mr Brodie came to my house just at the time the eight o'clock bell was ringing and he remained in it all night, and was not out from the time he came in until a little before nine o'clock next morning. We went to bed early, about ten o'clock, as Mr Brodie complained that night of being much indisposed with a sore throat.

Much was made of the presence of a 7-year-old son there at the time, who had been happy 'to see my daddie who has been in the house all night'.

What on earth would Anne Grant have thought of all this when, like the fascinated general public, she heard – presumably for the first time – about the other woman who had been taking such significant liberties with 'her' man?

Anne's reaction is not on record but it can be well imagined. Clearly she had not been short of Brodie's attention either, despite her greater distance from his general habitat, and as their eldest daughter Cecill – named after Brodie's mother – was 12 at the time of his trial, it is fair to assume that their relationship had been going on for at least that time. Was this without her knowing of the other woman? Perhaps he thought she might not be interested. In any case, young Cecill did manage to visit Brodie in prison just before he went to the gallows, and while final tender thoughts were exchanged between them, one wonders if there was also a message from her mother.

There is no doubt he loved them all, however, and ample evidence of that is in one of his letters written on the run to the stabler Michel Henderson (see chapter 5), in which he confesses himself 'very uneasy on account of Mrs Grant and my three children by her; they will miss me more than any other in Scotland' – and goes on to offer his opinion of who among them should do what with their future working lives.

He clearly loved them all, both the mistresses and their children by him, but what were the chances that such a wayward man could contain his affections to just two women in a city rampant with temptations? It is not hard to imagine how he would follow the mischievous devil on his left shoulder, when you consider how much the city's womanhood was admired even by less love-thirsty characters such as Dr Johnson's biographer James Boswell, who kept a mistress in Borthwick's Close, and by the aforementioned visitor (and product of Trinity College, Cambridge), Edward Topham.

'Love reconciles me to a Scotch accent which from the mouth of a pretty woman is simply and sweetly melodious', wrote Boswell, while Topham recorded that 'their hearts are soft and full of passion', adding, 'The younger women have a certain proportion of embonpoint and voluptuousness which makes them highly the objects of luxurious love.' Another visitor wrote of 'their noble walk' along the streets. But their charms, despite good Scottish complexions, were not achieved without some hard work. Here is a humorous writer's description of a fashionable young Scots lady of 1779:

> Give Betsy a bushel of horsehair and wool,
> Of paste and pomatum a pound;
> Ten yards of gay ribbon to deck her sweet skull,
> And gauze to encompass it round.
> Of all the bright colours the rainbow displays,
> Are these ribbons which hang from her head,
> And her flowers adapted to make the folk gay,
> For round the whole width are they spread.
> Her flaps fly behind for a yard at the least,
> And her curls meet just under her chin;
> And these curls are supported, to keep up the jest,
> With an hundred instead of one pin.
> Her gown is tucked up to the hip on each side,
> Shoes too high for a walk and a jump,
> And to deck the sweet creature complete for a bride,
> The cork-cutter has made her a rump.

Thus finished in taste, while on her I gaze,
I think I could take her for life;
But I fear to undress her, for out of her stays,
I should find I had lost half my wife.

How much would Brodie have been able to resist the wider range of such charms? Not much, it may be assumed. Especially if availability came down to purchasing power – which at times he had and other times hadn't. In any case, in 1775, when he was in his early 30s, sexually active and doing quite well, just three years before he became a rich man on the death of his father, a daring small book was published that riveted the attention of Edinburgh's young, and sometimes not-so-young, bucks. Sold discreetly for a shilling, with a preface by a celebrated wit of the time, it frankly described some fifty Edinburgh prostitutes, their bedtime talents and attributes and, most importantly for the contemporary connoisseur, their names, addresses and ages. It was entitled *Ranger's Impartial List of the Ladies of Pleasure of Edinburgh*.

Would Brodie have invested a shilling in this? Readers are free to draw their own conclusions. But here are a few examples from its sixty pages that would surely have raised at least one of the eyebrows under his high forehead:

Miss SUTHERLAND at Miss WALKER'S.
This Lady is an old veteran in the service, about 30 years of age, middle sized, black hair and complection, and very good teeth, but not altogether good-natured. By her long experience in business, which is about 12 years, she is mistress of her profession; she is a firm votary to the wanton Goddess, and would willingly play morning, noon, and night, at the delicious game of push-pin. As a friend, we will give a caution to this Lady, not to make free with a gentleman's pocket, especially when he is in liquor; as it was upon that account that Miss Forsyth put her away from her house, for which every person will commend her.

Miss WATT at MISS ADAMS'S

This lady is about 21 years of age of the middle size, light brown hair, good teeth, but rather surly in her temper, especially after the glass has gone merrily round; notwithstanding of this, she is not a bad companion, as she can sing many very fine songs. It is said, before she would sleep alone, she would rather pay a clever fellow to do her business, as love is her sole delight.

Miss GALLOWAY at Miss WALKER'S.

This Lady comes from the land of Blunders, and served her apprenticeship aboard a man of war, which probably may be the occasion that her temper is not so agreeable as one could wish. However, she is not contemptible in her profession, and she is well acquainted with the art of jostling. She will heave, twist and twine, when she is quite in play, with any nymph that ever sported in those pleasing groves dedicated to the Goddess Venus. She is about 24 years of age, thick and short, and of a fair complexion.

Miss GILMOR at Miss WALKER'S

This is a little thick Lady, about 20 years of age, brown hair, good skin and teeth, and pretty good natured. She is also very coy, and amorous to the greatest degree, and has courage enough (although little) not to be afraid of the largest and strongest man that ever drew weapon in the cause of love, upon that account she, for the most part, gives satisfaction.

Miss McCULLOCH at Mrs YOUNG'S

She is extremely loving, and gives great satisfaction in the Critical Minute, as all those declare who have had the pleasure of her embraces. She has got fine tempting legs, which she is not a little fond of showing, as she appears very often in men's clothes. Take her all in all, she is an agreeable companion.

Miss STEPHENSON at Miss WALKER'S

This Lady is also tall and thin, black hair, good teeth, bad eyes, but her good nature makes up for that deficiency. She is about 23 years of age, and very fond of that sport which all nature is inclined to. She is very eager in the Critical Minute, and would inspire the dullest mortal with joy and vigour, and if she knows any method to create fresh desire in her lover, she will willingly do it.

Mrs KETTY [Various aliases] at Mrs YOUNG'S

This Lady has had a great propensity for the Gentlemen of the Quill. She was also in keeping with a certain Baronet, but she has left his embrace for one of the former, who goes under the name of her husband. She is very good natured, artful in her amours; and it is said, that was the Devil himself to come in a golden shower, she would as soon meet his embrace as those of Jupiter.

Did he perhaps seek divine forgiveness occasionally for his transgressions? Apparently not. At a time when the Church was central to most people's lives, William Brodie seems not to have been much of a churchgoer – if the dates of some of his misadventures are anything to go by. Indeed, Sunday was a favourite day for getting up to no good, if only because many premises were vacated by the faithful while they went to worship. One of his biggest targets in his later career was a silk shop where, in preparation for an attack on it, he and an accomplice went frequently to test the stock-lock most commonly on Sunday mornings.

It was a Sunday when, with the help of a respectable but shocked cousin – concerned about the family honour – he stole secretly out of the city and country fearing the game was nearly up. And it was a Sunday too when one of his earliest robberies took place, when an old lady of his acquaintance (who should have been at church but had given it a miss) was politely relieved of her money.

That incident could be seen as part of a small series of experimental forays before his full shocking campaign was launched.

For there were several embryonic cases of errant behaviour and downright theft that were, with hindsight, surely perpetrated by him, but – until that major robbery spree began in August, 1786 – were not linked together by the authorities or even by the gossip-mongers to nip his activities in the bud. Despite plenty of reasons for suspicions.

The almost unbelievable audacity of the Sunday-morning robbing of that older woman was perhaps forced upon him by the realisation that, in what he thought would be an empty house, he was being watched. But it almost set a style for his being caught red-handed, in that the essential part of his disguise – the crepe mask – would create doubt in the victim's mind about the identity they suspected ('but it just couldn't have been him!') and the exercise was followed through so coolly that they might imagine they had been dreaming.

In any case, unable to go to church that day as she was feeling under the weather, the lady in question was also alone in her house, as her servant was absent on divine worship (as Brodie had calculated). She was suddenly awakened from a daydream and into what seemed like a bad dream – shocked by the entrance of a masked man into the room where she sat. Her mouth fell open in disbelief as he nodded to her, smiled and picked up a set of keys lying on the table in front of her. He then walked over to her bureau, opened a few drawers and relieved it of a 'considerable sum of money' (she later told a friend) that had been hidden away for safekeeping. Panic-stricken and paralysed during the whole incident, she was sure she recognised the housebreaker and her eyes were wide with a mixture of fear and disbelief as, after relocking the desk, he moved back over to her to replace the keys on the table. He then made a low bow, smiled again as a kind of polite thank you, and took his leave as calmly as he had entered. When he was gone and she calmed down, she exclaimed to herself, 'Surely that was Deacon Brodie!' But not even her closest friend would believe that someone of his respectability could have ever stooped so low as to turn burglar. The victim, for fear of embarrassment, never mentioned it again – until, presumably, the Deacon's crimes came fully to light.

These included another such early incident which brings to mind the comment of Robert Louis Stevenson that 'many a citizen was proud to welcome the Deacon to supper, and dismissed him with regret at a timeous hour, who would have been vastly disconcerted had he known how soon, and in what guise, his visitor returned'.

The story, as told by Stevenson, went like this. A friend of Brodie, who lived 'some way towards heaven' in one of the city's great lands (high buildings) had told him, during one such convivial supper, that he was intending to go out into the country and would be absent for some time. As it happened, however, his trip was delayed by his having to attend to some unexpected business, so he was still in town on the first night that he should have been absent. The business matters must have been rather complex and worrying, for he lay awake far into the small hours, according to the Tron church bell. And then …! Was he finally dreaming? He suddenly heard a creak and saw a faint light. Jumping as silently out of bed as he could, he dashed over to a false window that looked on to another room – and there he was sure he saw, illuminated by a hand-held lantern, his good friend William Brodie in a mask; who had presumably intended to take full advantage of the owner's lack of attendance to his valuables; and who, just like a bad dream, doused his flame and faded away into the dark …

What these dramas had in common was that, although Brodie was recognised in both of them, no official action was taken by his victims. In one instance the man was simply reluctant to incriminate his friend; in the other the old lady preferred to doubt the evidence of her own senses – a truly striking proof of the near-infinite advantages to be gained from a respectable family background. And didn't William Brodie know it.

It was remarkable that both these first modest toes-in-the-water of crime gave him a shocking caught-red-handed moment, yet at a highly sensitive time there came another example of his apparently fearless audacity – and of a merciless streak with regard to that family background that could truly take a good person's breath away. When his father, the much-respected Francis Brodie, succumbed to palsy at his house in the Lawnmarket on the evening of Saturday 1 June 1782, his playboy son was out gambling. And as Saturday merged into Sunday (that special day again), with his belated visit finally made while the old man's body was laid out with candles burning around it, the new head of the Brodie dynasty decided to set out on an endeavour that – he knew – would never be attributed by right-thinking folk to a grieving son.

He had prepared his raid on Thomson's, the High Street tobacconist, well. Having commissioned the Brodie firm three months before to build new shelves and drawers with brass handles to house his precious stock imported from all over the world, Mr Thomson had absented himself from the shop now and again to let the craftsmen get on unhindered. And at such moments it had occurred to Brodie more than once, especially when his men were off on an ale break, that there was more than just a world of fine tobaccos – Arabian Latakia, spicy Bahia Brazil, fire-cured Kentuck, chewable Burmese and high-quality Cuban, as well as the popular Virginia and snuffs galore – to admire here: there was the shop's main key hanging unguarded on a hook inside the door and positively inviting him to take a putty impression of it in his little japan-black box.

He had yielded to temptation then, taken the imprint with window putty, made a copy key from it, and now, having learned Mr Thomson was going away for some time, he decided to use it with a view to settling some urgent gambling debts. With a small smile of mischief playing about his narrow lips, he slowly shed his day street finery – the fine silken waistcoat, the light-coloured trousers and overcoat – and donned his chosen costume of the night: trousers and stockings, waistcoat, cloak and gloves, all in black. A bold macabre touch – his late father's crumpled wig of dark curls – almost completed the ensemble, except that when he came out of the shadows and descended into the Cowgate emporium of nicotiana about to make his entry, there would also be the black crepe mask. He stuffed the last two items into the deep cloak pockets along with a jemmy and a loaded pistol, while in his near-invisibility he carried his dark lantern along the street on one gloved hand with his home-made key in the other.

This he slipped quietly into the door's heavy lock and – as he glanced briefly about him to check no candles were suddenly flickering – it turned easily. Inside, all was familiar to him as a one-time work site and, while he helped himself to a raffia-tied bundle of cheroots, he even knew where Mr Thomson's money would be held. But alas! As he started forcing the relevant mahogany drawer open, while admiring the strength of his own handiwork, he heard the cry 'Who's there?' and wheeled round to see the night-gowned Thomson descending the stone stairs from his home to his shop, with a candle under his chin casting scary facial shadows. 'Thief!' Thompson cried.

Brodie instinctively went for his pistol but thought better of it and, as he quickly decided to avoid confrontation and promptly take his leave, he defaulted instead for the ironically polite response that was to become something of a Brodie farewell trademark. He bowed, doffed his hat and said 'Guid nicht to ye, Mr Thomson.'

Trembling with rage and shock, the tobacconist watched without following the dark little figure vanishing into the night, and when a member of the city guard finally answered his repeated calls of 'Thief!' and asked if he had recognised the robber, Mr Thomson held his tongue. But he knew there was something oddly familiar about the figure and voice of the arrogant masked man who had so nearly robbed him and damn near even shot him.

Brodie had got away with it again. And suitably impressed by his own talent for escaping firm identification and therefore justice, he reckoned – as he anticipated times getting tougher – that he would be getting down to this sort of thing in a much more serious and concentrated fashion in the not too distant future.

3

THE BIRTH OF
HIS CRIMINAL HALF

The sawdusty workshop in Brodie's Close attacked the senses and brought a smile to his fox-like face. It smelled of fresh wood, boiling fishy glue, resin and lacquer, and it sounded like a busy place: saws ripping, hammers banging, planes sighing, man-to-man shouting. And when he chose to honour it with his well-dressed presence and proffer expert advice over the craftsmen's apron-holding shoulders, the son of the house was companionable and professional enough to be seen as reasonable boss material. Not that he was near that point yet, but young William was getting into practice and, metaphorically at least, he was rubbing his hands in anticipation with plenty to smile about.

The birth of Edinburgh's New Town in 1767, when he was a tender 26, meant a new surge of business. For anyone skilled in the creation of furniture, what was to be a century-long development of classical homes on Edinburgh's northern fields marked a golden age of enviable prosperity. He was already feeling the benefits by sharing in his father Francis's growing workload when the old man died at 74 in 1782 – just as young James Craig's winning city-scape scheme, designed to transform reekie old Edinburgh into the Athens of the North, was getting into its elegant stride.

Waves of public and private money were being invested into the grand initiative of Provost George Drummond (little of which he would live to see realised) to attract not just the city's own professionals and aristocracy out of the overcrowded Old Town but expatriates 'of rank' who now saw, set against the claustrophobia of London, a breathable future amid the wide avenues and Doric, Ionic and Corinthian pillars of their own grand capital. Wealthy Scots riding a sudden wave of industrial enterprise in building, iron works, land ownership, law, banking, sugar and tobacco importation, brewing, publishing and commerce generally were gathering here to seek out new lives, new homes … and new furniture.

It meant that, on his father's death, William Brodie's legacy was multi-faceted: the means through inherited ownership of the family business and property to exploit that great tide of money-making opportunity; the aforementioned £10,000; and – perhaps most significant of all – his father's spotless reputation as an upstanding citizen and town councillor.

Some people sensed that differently, of course: for one, the old lady who had been visited by him and relieved of her money, politely, in the night; William Creech, the councillor and publisher whose High Street bookselling business was near enough the Brodie homestead to know him very well (of which more later); and William's own sisters, Jacobina and Jean, who knew him even better but had at least expected him to show up at his father's deathbed.

Yet the son who did not quite make it to the old widower's departure – who had been too busy sleeping off 'the night before' at a mistress's house – also received the benefit of any doubt. With his weaknesses and indiscretions hardly believed or recognised by wider society, he was seen as a chip off the old master craftsman and gentleman, who had been Deacon of the Incorporation of Wrights, cabinet-maker extraordinary and Mason of Lodge Kilwinning, Canongate. Surely William would be another safe pair of Brodie hands? And so, as night follows day, within a year the bereaved son was filling the father's shoes as a Deacon Councillor of the City, a position that gave him primary access to lucrative council projects in his field.

It seemed William Brodie had been left holding a whole handful of life's trump cards, which must have felt like quite a triumph for one so keen on gambling ...

So how would he play it? The safest bet would be to feign a furrowed brow of grief and hold all these cards close to his chest while relaxing into his perceived respectability and watching his potential customer base grow organically. But if the truth were known, his wayward soul was not enamoured of safety or respectability. He was cunning enough to present that face to the world for as long as possible, but under the shadow of his three-cornered hat there was a mischievous if calculating brain that sought the darker side of life, that ached for illegitimate adventure. He would, of course, try to keep it well hidden while he enjoyed the fruits of his inheritance, but he no doubt sensed that that would be finite – as indeed it proved to be.

Though he enjoyed the fruits of the New Town's demands, one thing he wouldn't do with his new-found fortune was join the gentry's exodus to the north. His life was intensely centred around the Old Town and he sensed that it would survive and even thrive. For even before the coming of the New Town, the city had been gaining post-Culloden confidence. New banks had appeared to service government and the landed gentry and support burgeoning industries such as engineering and shipbuilding, coal, iron and cotton. But to put the icing on the cake, rising alongside the elegantly ordered New Town, with its royal street-name tributes and King George III's personal endorsement, was the city's new international reputation as 'a hotbed of genius', home to the leaders of a new wave of ideas known as the Scottish Enlightenment. The city's intellectual buzz was encapsulated in this memorable comment attributed to the King's Chemist, Englishman John Amyatt, talking in the mid-1700s: 'Here I stand, at what is called the Cross of

Edinburgh, and can, in a few minutes, take fifty men of genius and learning by the hand.'

The Cross? He meant the fourteenth-century Mercat Cross, part of which still stands in Parliament Square within an elaborate Victorian base built in 1885, the landmark where royal proclamations and other official announcements were read out, where merchants and citizens – and enlightened figures – gathered to talk and exchange ideas. As such, the area of the Cross was still the city's hub, focus of most of that new cultural consciousness – despite the developing New Town. For while Craig's architectural masterpiece (now a World Heritage site) created the kind of living space that the Old Town had lacked, forced as it had been to expand ever upwards with unhealthy, packed-out, reach-for-the-sky tenements, the new scheme had taken on the nature of a social experiment – successful in many respects but with the socially divisive effect of separating rich and poor as never before. Its exclusivity was threatening to create sealed-off lifestyles that would erode inter-class relationships.

The privileged professionals in the newly gentrified north could not be totally isolated, however, as there was a conspicuous shortage of commercial premises and caterings for basic human needs in this well-gardened residential plan: then, as now to some extent, it had relatively few shops, taverns, workshops, hotels or clubs and minimal general social buzz. So with little in the way of fine goods, furnishings and social contact immediately to hand in their still-growing community, this higher society began to regard the Old Town – before Princes Street emerged with luxury shops and products to satisfy their new expectations – as a place to revisit. Not just for shopping and snuff but for the intellectual stimulation of the Enlightenment magnet personified by people like the philosopher David Hume, the economist Adam Smith and, of course, the most intriguing draw of them all, Ayrshire's ploughman poet Robert Burns, lured to 'Edina' in 1786 to be celebrated as 'Caledonia's Bard' for his revised edition of *Poems, Chiefly in the Scottish Dialect*.

Grand personages invited the handsome bard-in-buck-skin-breeches to their homes for him to be regarded with wonder – especially by much-impressed ladies. In reciprocal tribute, and thinking for a moment that he ought to be posh in the manner of his well-born admirers, he briefly abandoned his Ayrshire roughage to write a less-than-successful 'English' tribute to the capital whose eight verses began with:

> Edina! Scotia's darling seat!
> All hail thy palaces and tow'rs;
> Where once, beneath a Monarch's feet,
> Sat Legislation's sovereign pow'rs:
> From marking wildly-scatt'red flow'rs,
> As on the banks of Ayr I stray'd,
> And singing, lone, the ling'ring hours,
> I shelter in thy honour'd shade.

As it happened, Burns's lodging in Scotia's darling seat was in Baxter's Close (near today's Writers' Museum in Lady Stair's Close), almost immediately opposite Deacon Brodie's premises in the cobbled Lawnmarket. And while the star visitor was making a raft of illustrious local contacts like the Earl of Glencairn, distinguished lawyer Henry Erskine and *Encyclopaedia Britannica* editor William Smellie, not to mention the celebrated painters Nasmyth and Raeburn, it is said that the two near-neighbours became acquainted and that Brodie even attended the party at which Burns met, and was smitten by, Clarinda, his unfulfilled love and poetic inspiration.

The men certainly shared at least one drinking den: Johnnie Dowie's, a dark but convivial alcove of a tavern in Libberton's Wynd (the now-demolished address of Brodie's mistress Jean Watt, roughly locatable today as the east pavement of George IV Bridge), where in a long narrow backroom affectionately dubbed The Coffin the poet would hold court on matters political and romantic among his admirers.

These included a mutual acquaintance, William Creech, the staunchly moralistic bookseller-publisher of Burns's Edinburgh edition who, as a fellow town councillor and another near neighbour, was always wary of Brodie. Creech was to have his suspicions confirmed when he served on the jury at the famous burglar's trial, and he then published his own musings on the event, printed just days later. He was also a co-founder of Edinburgh's Speculative Society, a debating club whose members included various great figures such as Francis Horner and Sir Walter Scott.

So the Old Town remained the city's beating heart, despite its continuing squalor in places, and could not be written off by the gradual coming to life of James Craig's great vision. Not only was the city's ancient centre a stage for 'all human life is there' day-to-day theatre, it had, along its fishlike High Street backbone with closes shooting off like ribs on either side, thriving retail premises and offices, clubs and tobacconists, booksellers and busy workshops, such as that of the Brodies. With the great lowering castle at its top end and the delicately handsome French-style Palace of Holyroodhouse at the lower end, the Royal Mile also had close proximity to other important buildings, such as the university and law courts, and – one that figures fatefully in this tale – the General Excise Office for Scotland in Chessel's Court off the Canongate.

None of these cultural developments, prestigious buildings or changing circumstances would have been missed by the calculating 41-year-old Brodie, who now began to weigh up his future prospects in the light of his new-found fortunes.

He might have survived into his forties as an apparently reputable and prosperous man of some standing in the community, but he knew his place in that scheme of things and had no aspiration to join the gentry's exodus over the relatively new North Bridge now spanning the drained gulf that had been the Nor' Loch, the stinking near-sewer under the castle that would later become the fragrant Princes Street Gardens; no, he was a fixture in the familiar Old Town, where he would live out his life to the bitter end – literally, as it turned out. Not just because of the intrusive nature of his work, he knew who and what lay down every close and behind every door and would only occasionally step outside of its familiar mile-long stream of humanity.

For what? He was easily tempted by betting opportunities, so, as a breeder and owner of fighting cocks, he could often be found at Henderson's Stables in the Grassmarket cheering on his own feathered champions. He also loved tavern card and dice games and, while often losing, would go to extraordinary lengths to win, yielding to the temptation to cheat – and not just against the chimney sweep who formally accused him of foul play. Losing did not sit well with Brodie, and his resulting fits of depression would drive him straight to his favourite antidote therefor: alcohol.

Relax into his respectability? After the reading of his father's will, it initially seemed to him that his dissolute nightlife might slip into the past, but his other darker half sensed that this was self-delusion; that there could only be one eventual consequence of his good fortune. With immediate financial concerns lifted from his shoulders he succumbed to the weaker side of his character and the recreational enjoyments of spending unwisely. He slowly began to realise, however, that 'recreational' has a way of getting serious …

Then there were his two most expensive obligations: a pair of mistresses (see chapter 2) and their broods who required keeping in the manner to which they had become accustomed. That meant an expectation that when rents and food threatened to be unpayable he would be standing ready to bear his (what a word for him) responsibility.

Despite his business going relatively well, with his privileged access to council work and high demand from wealthy private clients, it began to dawn on him that his after-hours lifestyle could not be maintained on what he could earn legally, even with the help of his fast-diminishing inheritance, and that something would inevitably have to give.

The process would, of course, take time, the aforementioned factors gradually combining over something like six years with other negatives – huge gaming debts, a taste for late-night drinking and out-of-bounds women – to create the perfect financial storm. Though unable or unwilling to tame himself, he finally saw that his new life could only end one way, and, with his double personality working overtime, his 'respectable' side could not abide the thought of bankruptcy. By 1786 he had decided that a new tack was urgently needed, and it would have to be about generating enough income. This was the catalytic acceptance that marked the birth of William Brodie's active criminal half.

In many ways his life had been already divided into two, as contrasting as night and day: the neat, tidy and superficially charming man who walked and talked his way around the city's transparent daytime world of hearty greetings, respectable social contact, deals and dealmakers and his opposing night-time world of flickering street lanterns, dark closes, drunken trysts, dubious motivations, violence and shady contacts.

Though it was at first a secret only to himself, this darker half that he feigned to struggle with but really relished was about to take over his life. It had occurred to him in the course of his legitimate work – the making of cabinets with doors and house or office doors themselves – that if he had not fitted them himself, he had exclusive access to some clients' keys, having a whole selection either directly to hand or being able to find and copy them. And while the conclusion of this thought was fully forming, a double opportunity was presenting itself. The council had decided, with the inclusion of his vote, to clear away the ancient cobbles of the High Street and lower its overall level, with the attendant need to replace doors (often with new locks) – which was, almost literally, just up Brodie's street. So many keys! So many chances to access other people's premises! It was more than such an easily tempted man could resist.

There is no record of whether the Deacon battled with his conscience at this point, but one suspects not; if he had such a thing, he might have paid it lip service, but all the evidence suggests he was romantically excited about his new 'naughty' choice of direction; that he saw it as a kind of (nicely lucrative) sport. And so it all began, the long series of sinister house and shop break-ins that suddenly gripped the city centre and deeply puzzled it too. Some places were entered with so little disturbance and damage that many people began to think there was some supernatural power at work.

For Brodie the delicious irony of it all was that – while making all the right shocked noises to the victims and acquaintances about such 'outrageous' thefts – he himself was benefiting from alarmed property-owners asking for increased security in the form of stronger doors and better locks.

So what were the offending incidents? Not considering earlier events suspected of being his work, such as the daylight robbery of an old lady and that of Thomson's tobacconist shop just after his father died in 1780 (see the previous chapter), the main series happened some six years later. This consisted of eleven break-ins in all, the first perpetrated by Brodie himself who, on such expeditions, always carried a shaded lantern and sometimes a pistol (or two), and dressed in a crepe mask and dark clothes. He made his first mistake when he began to work with three dubious accomplices.

First to be recruited – as a daytime locksmith for the Brodie workshop as well as an aide in nocturnal projects – was a Berkshire refugee called George Smith, who had come to Scotland with his wife and horse-drawn cart in mid-1786 and taken shelter at the Grassmarket stables of Michael Henderson, which accommodated not just horses and fighting cocks but (according to one historian) 'the lower order of travellers'.

Being around there a lot to cheer on his feathered friends, William Brodie soon made Smith's acquaintance and noted not just his dire circumstances but also his professed skills as a locksmith. With his physical and financial health going rapidly downhill, the Englishman had had to sell his horse and cart to pay his rent, so – Brodie reckoned – he would no doubt be open to 'ideas' to improve his lot. Having accordingly groomed him with friendly conversation, Brodie eventually broached the possibility of 'something being done to advantage, provided a due degree of caution is exercised' – and did not have to ask twice. The 'doing of something' was clearly nothing new or particularly daunting to Smith, who, having had his expertise with locks well tested by Brodie, was quickly brought on board – and just as quickly improved his lot by setting up home and a suitable 'front' as small grocery shop in the Cowgate. He often accompanied his boss to his favourite den of iniquity, Clark's gambling house in Fleshmarket Close, where, over well-lubricated card games, they both befriended the other two recruits: Andrew Ainslie, sometime shoemaker in Edinburgh, and another Englishman-on-the-run, John Brown, who often called himself Humphrey Moore. They occupied a lodging together at the foot of Burnet's Close.

Two Scots and two Englishmen, stretching across several strata of society. But what they had in common was the fact that each was a misfit in one way or another. Such a motley little army needed a little general, and, after doing the first 'job' himself, Brodie began to revel in that role as project-planning became increasingly precise and sophisticated. Indeed, the job description for Smith should have included 'opportunities to travel' for part of the operation became fencing off certain acquired articles – such as the proceeds from goldsmith John Tapp's house and the silver mace from the university – as far away as was practicable. This meant getting to Chesterfield where 'expelled' Scot John Tasker (alias Murray) was the only-too-willing receiver of such goods for selling at his Bird in Hand shop. And it meant at least one long Brodie-funded coach trip back to his homeland for George Smith, who must have thought – perversely – that he had come up in the world since crossing the border with his horse and cart so relatively recently.

The timeline of their misdeeds – or their crimeline, if you like – began in mid-1786 and went like this:

12 August: The outer door of Messrs Johnston and Smith, bankers in the Royal Exchange, is opened – presumably by a counterfeit key – and over £800 taken from the drawers. Most notes are from the big three banks of the time, Bank of Scotland, Royal Bank and British Linen. Messrs Johnston and Smith resolve to fight for the money's recovery, denouncing the 'wicked persons' responsible and announcing, through the *Edinburgh Evening Courant*, that a good reward is being offered – £5 for every £100 recovered with the help of any informer. This need not be an involved party, it is suggested, 'as some smith may very innocently have made an impression of clay or wax, such smith giving information, so as the person who got the key may be discovered, shall be handsomely rewarded'.

9 October: The Parliament Close shop of goldsmith James Wemyss loses fifty gold and diamond rings, brooches and earrings, also a whole variety of valuable spoons. In reporting the story, the *Courant* issues a warning to other such shopkeepers, writing: 'As the public, as well as the private party, are greatly interested that this daring robbery be discovered, it is requested that all Goldsmiths, Merchants and other Traders throughout Scotland, may be attentive in case any goods answering to those above-mentioned shall be offered for sale.' A ten-guinea reward offered by the Incorporation of Goldsmiths 'upon conviction of the offender or offenders' attracts no interest and is assumed (too late) to have been too modest.

November: Bridge Street hardware merchants McKain's has clearly been broken into – the lock that should have kept out intruders has been breached – and loses seventeen steel watch-chains in what is later revealed by Smith to have been a practice run for the real thing a fortnight later. This is thwarted in mid-burglary by Smith hearing 'a person in the room immediately below rise out of his bed' causing him to run 'straight into the street' and be off with a waiting Brodie, so nothing appears to have been stolen.

8 December: The shop of John Law, tobacconist in the Exchange, is broken into, and a canister containing between £10 and £12 carried off. This robbery, though not confessed to later by any of their gang, is probably the work of Smith and Brodie.

Christmas Eve: From their shop at the corner of Bridge Street and High Street – just opened, with a new door and lock fitted – a distressed John and Andrew Bruce report that several gold and silver watches and rings worth £350 have gone missing in the night. This has been a solo job by Smith, unable to prise its setter-up Brodie away from a gambling winning streak. Press reports, telling of a twenty-guinea reward for information, point out that all the rings bear the shop's mark, so it is perhaps surprising that Brodie's acceptance of some token items from the haul should include two rings. It is agreed between the two that Smith should go to Chesterfield to dispose of the goods to their fence, banished Scot John Tasker, and Brodie gives five and a half guineas to pay the fare.

Christmas Day: Another reason for a trip down south: Goldsmith John Tapp is relieved of valuable items from his broken-into home while being detained at his Parliament Close shop by a bottle-wielding John Brown on the pretext of having a merry seasonable drink. Items taken by Brodie and the others include eighteen guinea notes, a 20s note, a silver watch, some rings, his pocket book and the well-hidden gold frame of a gentleman's picture belonging to his wife. Some reports say that, on being confronted by her, Brodie talks his way out of the situation by saying he knows the sex-hungry man in the picture and wouldn't her husband like to know him too …

(Note that most of this was happening around the same Old Town area, but in an unexpected geographic change, the next job took place in Leith. This was apparently instigated by Smith, who had been 'feeling the pinch' after a pause in their programme caused by a shaken Brodie's sudden reversal into a period of respectability and only legitimate business.)

August 1787: Grocer John Carnegie of Leith loses a huge quantity of fine black tea and, oddly, some of it is recovered when tea-packed parcels are found along the length of the road from Leith to Edinburgh. It is assumed that the burglars, not being in the prime of fitness, have found the weight of the goods, combined with the distance of the walk back to the city, literally too much to bear.

29 October: The burglars return to their comfort zone in the heart of the city with a raid on a fashionable shoemaker's shop in Royal Exchange. Losses may have been light as they are not recorded.

30 October: Recovering their taste for the audacious, the Brodie gang is responsible for the disappearance of the college mace – a three-century-old silver masterpiece – from the library in the quad of Edinburgh University. While this much-lamented precious symbol also makes its way to Chesterfield, another appeal goes out to the criminal fraternity: 'A reward of ten guineas, to be paid by the City Chamberlain, is hereby offered for the discovery of all or any of the persons responsible.'

9 January 1788: The silk shop of Messrs Inglis and Horner loses £500 worth of cambrics, satins and silks. The Procurator Fiscal puts up £100 reward, later increased to £150, and promises a free pardon for any accomplice turning king's evidence. His offer reads:

Whereas, upon the night of the 8th or morning of the 9th of January instant, the shop of Messrs Inglis Horner & co, Silk Mercers in Edinburgh, was broke into, and articles taken therefrom amounting to upwards of £300 value; and as the persons guilty of this robbery have not as yet been discovered, notwithstanding every exertion that has been made, and the offer of £100 of reward for that purpose, his Majesty's most gracious pardon is hereby offered to an accomplice, if there was more than one concerned, who shall, within six months from this date, give such information to William Scott, Procurator-Fiscal for the shire of Edinburgh, as shall be the means of apprehending and securing all or any of the persons guilty of or accessory to the said crime.

5 March 1788 is to be a fateful date with destiny, however; the night of the botched final job that starts the downfall of the man who thought he could cheat people, justice and even death. The target is nothing less than Scotland's General Excise Office …

★★★

Was it something to sing about? Now things were getting deadly serious. This was the most audacious criminal enterprise tried in Scotland so far, by this gang or any other: an attack on the very revenues of the nation. And a tipsy Brodie came thoroughly equipped – an hour late – to the gang's rendezvous at Smith's house. He wore an old-fashioned dark greatcoat, a black cocked hat and a black wig. He carried a dark lantern, a rope to tie up the old watchman who might get in their way, crepe masks for all four of them, a whistle for Ainslie as sentinel to communicate 'danger' in codes and a key that would fit the heavy main door.

Where and how did he get his hands on that? Having once visited the Excise Office with a friend from Stirling – a Mr Corbett who wanted to withdraw some money – Brodie had taken note of the layout of the place and was, inevitably, interested in the fact that it held an endless store of good citizens' cash; so much so that he resolved to know it even better and made several more visits as if doing business there – once with George Smith. That was when he saw the key of the outer door hanging on a nail and had Smith create a diversion while he quickly produced a handful of putty to make an impression of it. The resulting replica was successfully tested on a trial break-in a few nights before the scheduled Big Night.

For that event, apart from the key, the rope, the lantern, the masks and the whistle, several more interesting tools were brought to hand: some smaller keys and a double picklock, a pair of curling irons, an iron crowbar and the stolen coulter of a plough, selected for its heavy-duty leverage strength in challenging circumstances. But of all the items on hand at Smith's house on that night the most contentious was a number of loaded pistols, some borrowed from Michael Henderson of the Grassmarket stables.

How many were there? Some accounts say 'a brace', others 'two brace'. But one man on the spot had more precise information, dragged from his fevered memory during his erstwhile boss's subsequent trial. Ainslie said: 'I had no arms myself, excepting a stick, but Smith had three loaded pistols. Brown two, and Brodie one. At least, I saw Brodie, when he came into Smith's house, have one in his hand.'

The acquiring of weak playmates – it would soon transpire – represented a big mistake in Brodie's criminal career. But the acquiring of guns was even more fateful; probably his most reckless mistake ever. For their life-threatening potential could well have had a critical bearing on his own life. Burglary was one thing, the potential to kill quite another, perhaps even enough to justify, in those less-forgiving times, a sentence of death. His shocked colleagues certainly recognised that. But did he? Oblivion tomorrow was the last thing on his unhinged mind tonight, while he felt buzzing with aliveness, even as the others berated him for his lateness and looked askance at the pistols. They were obviously nervous, he thought, so he would try to cheer them up. Wearing one of the masks and brandishing one of the borrowed pistols, the respected dean of wrights and town councillor now looked more like a mad highwayman in a state of high excitement as he started singing to his grumpy colleagues these lines from *The Beggar's Opera*:

Let us take the road
Hark! I hear the sound of coaches!
The hour of attack approaches;
To your arms, brave boys, and load.
See the ball I hold;
Let the chymists toil like asses –
Our fire their fire surpasses,
And turns our lead to gold

Cheered up a little they might have been, but they were still nervous, and as their odd little band made their heavily laden way down the Canongate towards Chessel's Court at about 8 p.m. – minus Ainslie who had gone ahead as the look-out with his whistle – they could not have imagined just how badly wrong this final enterprise was about to go. No fewer than three factors would expose the sheer folly of it. This newspaper report tells the general story:

Excise Office Broke Into and Robbed

On the night betwixt the 5th and 6th of March, it is reported that some persons did feloniously enter the Excise Office by means of false keys and other implements, including the coulter of a plough, which has been discovered on the premises. The loss from the Office is not known for sure at this time but seems slight, the criminals having failed to gain access to secret drawers containing, it is reliably reported, more than eight hundred pounds Sterling. In breaking the front door a false key was used as is evident by the lack of any damage and its being open. The inner doors and the cashiers' desks however have suffered the most severe abuse under the hands of these criminals so that much expense will be required to repair the Offices and make them safe.

Mr James Bonnar of the Excise Office discovered the criminals in the very act of theft. Indeed, if he had not fortunately returned to his office, disturbing them, they might yet have found the great sum of money no matter how well it had been hid. Mr Bonnar has made a full report of his information regarding this terrible crime to the Sheriff-Clerk's Office and the Advertisement relating to it is expected daily. This crime seems to be one more in the never-ending attacks on the property and reputation of our city to which we have recently been laid open. The Magistracy has undertaken to discuss the matter and see what further precautions may be under-taken to deter such persons as will consider such a crime as robbing His Gracious Majesty's Excise.

But the devil was in the detail. The three factors that conspired against them were largely human: the unexpected appearance of bank official Bonnar, the disappointment at their minimal haul (about £16 when they were expecting something like £1,000) and the consequent bitter effect on Brown, their already discontented and disaffected accomplice who had been feeling left out of several jobs and, being on the run from a transportation sentence for a crime committed in England, was becoming ever more ready to take up the Procurator Fiscal's offer of a free pardon. Not to mention the offered reward, from the earlier silk job, of £150.

But to capture the drama of the Excise Office break-in at the handsome (and still standing) Chessel's Building, we are grateful for the two imagined scenes conjured up by author Forbes Bramble and his 1975 book *The Strange Case of Deacon Brodie*. Crepe-masked Smith and Brown, having forced their way in and over to the cashier's door with the aid of false keys and 'the splintering efficiency of the coulter and wedges', lit their lantern and tapers, then produced the toupee tongs to make short work of the desks. But they overlooked a concealed drawer in one of them that contained a good £600.

'There's no bloody money!' Brown was almost frothing at the mouth. 'That's your friend the Deacon!

'There's no bloody money!'

Drawers were strewn everywhere, and the raw edges of splintered wood shone white in the light of tapers.

'He saw it come in. It's here somewhere. Stow your lumber and keep looking.'

They started to re-search the desks, hunting for secret drawers. An exclamation from Brown brought Smith over.

'Here's something anyway!' He pulled out a purse and they counted its contents. 'Sixteen pounds! God Almighty, is that what we've risked a cropping for!'

And the witness? At first, Mr Bonnar – having returned to collect papers he needed for the morning – did not apparently appreciate what he had seen, assuming that it was a cheeky clerk barging past him.

> Pushing open the door and beating the snow from his boots, he was startled by the door suddenly hurtling back in his face, to be immediately thrust open while a figure in black hurtled out into the night, knocking him against the wall. These young clerks had been told about their behaviour.
>
> 'You!' he shouted. 'How dare you! Have you no manners, man? In this building you walk. It's as well I can't see you, I'd have you dismissed!' His yells were lost to the Close for the figure [Brodie] had already gone.

It all happened before Ainslie could blow his whistle, but he joined the escapee, and so did Smith and Brown, who had cocked their pistols as they followed Bonnar's footsteps but made their getaway whenever they sensed the coast to be relatively clear. The evening had not ended well and it was going to get worse. Not that Brodie was around to be confronted. While the others had gathered at Fraser's tavern in the New Town, where recriminations flew like wildfire flames, Brodie had slunk over to Jean Watt's house, not only for some comfort but also to give himself an alibi.

It was only after what happened next that Mr Bonnar put two and two together to realise just what (and perhaps who) he had literally bumped into at the office that night.

★★★

The next day they gathered at Smith's house-cum-grocery shop in the Cowgate, where his wife was presumably so uninterested she left the room. For he was to claim she had always been ignorant of his criminal way of life. The others were equally uninterested – and unimpressed – by Brodie's excuses and desperate promises of better projects in the pipeline, and Brown waited only to collect his £4 share of the Excise Office loot before he made his way to the Sheriff-Clerk's office. All he needed to convince William Middleton he was telling the truth was to take him – and a recruited Procurator Fiscal – up to the foot of Salisbury Crags in the dead of night and show them, under a lifted stone, the gang's stash of false keys. He also revealed the names of his fellow-accomplices, so that the fiscal ordered the sheriff-clerk to 'make the necessary arrangements to apprehend our friend's companions, Ainslie and Smith'.

For reasons known only to himself – was he contemplating blackmail? – Brown kept his powder dry on the naming and shaming of Deacon Brodie. If such a thought could be communicated to Ainslie and Smith and they also agreed to hold their tongues before being swept off to the Tolbooth prison, it would be, would it not, the perfect revenge against Brodie and his hopeless adventures? Meal tickets for life, assuming there would be an ongoing life.

It was when Brodie himself attempted to visit them in jail, no doubt to wheedle out a hint on whether or not his name had been mentioned, that he began to sense that it had. Despite his do-you-know-who-I-am entreaties to the two guards on duty, he was firmly told that no visitors, however important, were being allowed in. He sensed an unusual disrespect there and it was becoming rapidly clear to him that the game was almost up.

What he didn't yet know was that, as well as Brown and Ainslie, Smith had come clean and in his declarations had confessed to the robbery of the college mace, of Tapp's home, of a tea shop in Leith and also of the shop of Inglis and Horner. Smith also disclosed the extensive robbery committed on the shop of the Bruces and revealed that Brodie had been a participant in almost all the aforementioned thefts. Reported by the authorities thus:

Brodie told the declarant that the shop at the head of Bridge Street, belonging to Messrs Bruce, would be a proper shop for breaking into, as it contained valuable goods; and he knew the lock would be easily opened, as it was a plain lock, his men having lately altered that shop door at the lowering of the street: that the plan of breaking into the shop was accordingly concerted betwixt them ...

(While in prison, Smith and Ainslie made a desperate bid to escape on the night of 4–5 May by converting the iron handle of a bucket into a pick-lock and one of the iron hoops into a saw. Smith took one door off the hinges and opened the other, which led to Ainslie's cell upstairs. Both prisoners then cut a hole in the ceiling and another in the roof, ready to descend with the aid of sixteen fathoms of rope made out of bedsheets. They were foiled, however, by falling slates on the street attracting a sentinel, who raised the alarm.)

Later, while awaiting execution in the Tollbooth and wishing to make his peace with his maker, Smith revealed too that, had they not been stopped where they were, the Brodie gang would have gone on even more audaciously to cause much more damage and alarm. With his own hand, he drew up a list of targets – some of them quite major – that had been earmarked for future robberies. Plans in place for the remainder of 1788 had included the plundering of the Stirling stagecoach for the £1,000 workers' pay it would be carrying, the burglary of watchmakers Dalgleish and Dickie, lottery office-keepers White and Mitchell, a linen draper's in the Lawnmarket, 'a rich baker' near Brodie's Close and – demonstrating Brodie's imagination as well as his fearlessness – the Bank of Scotland. But even more daring was their intention to raid the Town Council Chamber for the mace below which the Deacon had sat for many a council meeting.

In any event, Brodie was now a hunted man, and he knew it. Staying in town was not an option. There was nothing for it but to make his getaway: to pack up fast and go as far away as possible. He would grab the first southbound coach, lose himself in London for a while, then perhaps head for the Continent; from there, on finding a suitable ship, he would head for America and anonymity. What an escape! An entirely new life would be awaiting him there – where no one, hopefully, would ever see the notices circulated by the Sheriff Clerk's Office that made all Edinburgh gasp with astonishment:

TWO HUNDRED POUNDS OF REWARD

Whereas WILLIAM BRODIE, a considerable house carpenter and burgess of the city of Edinburgh, has been charged with being concerned in breaking into the General Excise Office for Scotland, and stealing from the Cashier's office there a sum of money – and as the said William Brodie has either made his escape from Edinburgh, or is still concealed about that place – a REWARD of ONE HUNDRED AND FIFTY POUNDS STERLING is hereby offered to any person who will produce him alive at the Sheriff Clerk's Office, Edinburgh, or will secure him, so that he may be brought there within a month from this date; and FIFTY POUNDS STERLING MORE payable upon his conviction, by William Scott, procurator fiscal for the shire of Edinburgh.

James Bonnar was now pretty sure of just who had bustled past him at the Excise Office that fateful night.

4

ESCAPE – AND CAPTURE

Relief and regret, relief and regret. The clattering rhythm of the bouncing post chaise taking him further and further away from his shocked home town on that fateful Sunday – 9 March 1788 – must have driven like hammer blows into William Brodie's scrambled brain of mixed feelings. As John Gibson reported in his admirable account of Brodie's life, 'while Edinburgh was at its stint of Sunday morning devotion within the walls of St Giles, under the Dutch steeple of the Tron Kirk and in the Kirk of the Greyfriars, the Deacon was off down the Canongate, past the pleasure garden of Comely Green, and whirling through East Lothian'.

He was hoping to reach London and a new life within sixty hours for a fare-and-accommodation outlay of about five guineas; he couldn't deny that he had left a seriously damaged old life behind, and – a good reason for relief – had apparently escaped the consequences by the skin of his teeth. Immediately before this psychological turmoil there had been an equally intense perfect storm of preparation. In an age without telephonic communication, one can only wonder at how he got through it all in the few hours after making his decision to leave. There were allies to convince of his innocence, to brief and get help from: his cousin Milton, who would prime and pay a London lawyer to receive him there, and the Revd Nairn, who would likewise set up an American clergyman to help him on arrival in New York; not to mention the hiding of any evidence of his misdeeds, the organisation of clothes, money, books and introduction letters inside his big black travelling trunk, and the fond, 'forever' farewells to his two illegitimate families. There were many personal reasons for his regrets, but the last was surely the most poignant. And by the Monday, though he had barely left Newcastle, he was already haunted by a feeling of being alone, branded and hounded. What was now happening back home? He could only imagine with dread. And it was quite a lot ...

The news was well and truly out. With the procurator fiscal's £200 reward notice having already drawn scandalised gasps from the citizenry, Brodie's conspicuous absence from the scene ignited a veritable blaze of outraged gossip, just as a team of justice officers began to search his house in Brodie's Close – where the hiding of evidence had obviously not been thorough enough. Led by Brodie's old accomplice George Smith, hoping for leniency from the justice system in return for his cooperation, they found there the fleeing ring leader's dark lantern, several pick-locks and a parcel of twenty-five false keys, 'of uncommon construction', in a yard where his game cocks were kept. They also discovered the lidded japan-black case full of putty that he carried around to take impressions of his friends' door keys. Few would, or could, now deny Brodie's complicity. Who but he had had access to such keys by fitting new locks to the High Street shops when its new causeway was laid? But more damning than all of that were the two pistols discovered 'wrapped in a green cloth under the earth in the fireplace of a shade in the yard'.

Such finds dramatically reinforced the case against Brodie as they lined up with others revealed by Smith, who had also taken sheriff officers to an old dyke at the foot of Warriston's Close, under which they were shown some of the tools the gang had used to attack the Excise Office: the iron crowbar christened 'Little Samuel', toupee tongs and a false key for the front door.

No doubt about it. Everyone, including the man himself, now knew the game was up. And as if to formally confirm it, the following passage soon appeared in the *Edinburgh Evening Courant*, penned apparently by bookseller-publisher William Creech, Brodie's ever-suspicious council colleague:

The depredations that have been committed by housebreakers in and about this city for this some time past have been no less alarming than the art with which they have been executed, and the concealment that has attended them has been surprising. From a discovery, however, just made, there is reason to hope that a stop will soon be put to such acts of atrocious villainy. With what amazement must it strike every friend to virtue and honesty to find that a person is charged with a crime of the above nature who very lately held a distinguished rank among his fellow-citizens?

With what pity and compunction must we view the unfortunate victim who falls a sacrifice to justice for having violated the laws of his country, to which violation he was perhaps impelled by necessity, when rank, ease, and opulence are forfeited in endeavouring to gratify the most sordid avarice? For to what other cause than avarice can we impute the late robbery committed upon the Excise Office, when the situation of the supposed perpetrator is considered? No excuse from necessity can be pled for a man in the enjoyment of thousands, who will run the risk of life, honour, and reputation in order to attain the unlawful possession of what could in a very trifling degree add to his supposed happiness. See the advertisement from the Sheriff-Clerk's Office [*reproduced in the previous chapter*].

So where was Brodie fleeing to? According to a later-disclosed letter to his brother-in-law, his eventual intention was to reach New York where that American clergyman, primed by his Scottish colleague, would gather him up. The letter ended: 'Let my name and destination be a profound secret for fear of bad consequences.'

The hounding actually began on the Tuesday, when George Williamson, King's Messenger for Scotland, was ordered to track down Brodie and, after vainly checking out his known Edinburgh haunts, set off along London Road to learn from coachmen and post-boys along the route that the fugitive had made his way to the southern capital via Dunbar, Newcastle and York, latterly on the Flying Mercury light coach. From that vehicle's coachman he learned that Brodie (obviously already being cautious) had disembarked in London at the foot of Old Street, Moorfields, instead of going all the way to the Bull and Mouth terminus.

That was where the trail went cold for Williamson, though before giving up after eighteen days – and blaming himself – he had checked out most of London's 'billiard tables, hazard tables, cock-pits, tennis courts and other likely places' and, acting on information that Brodie was making for the Continent, 'pushed my inquiries as far as Margate, Deal and Dover in expectation of seeing him' – but simply didn't. Oddly enough, though, he had been right on the scent and only a few metres away from his quarry a couple of times as Brodie later reported that he saw Williamson twice 'but although countrymen usually shake hands when they meet from home, yet I did not choose to make so free with him, *notwithstanding he brought a letter to me*'.

This was confirmed at Brodie's subsequent trial when Williamson – speaking as a witness – revealed that he had some knowledge of a London lawyer-contact of Brodie's called William Walker and had even visited him during his quest at the suggestion of the now alerted and very interested Sir Sampson Wright, chief magistrate at Bow Street justice office, 'at whose desire I called upon Mr Walker, solicitor-at-law in the Adelphi, and inquired for Mr Brodie. He told me he was bad, and that I could not see him. I said I had a letter for him and wanted only to deliver it; but Mr Walker replied that it might perhaps be dangerous to allow me to see him.'

The extent of the Bow Street Runners' interest in the runaway Scot was confirmed by the latter himself, who said later: 'I saw my picture [his description in newspapers] exhibited to public view, and my intelligence of what was doing at Bow Street Office was as good as ever I had in Edinburgh.'

Brodie also confessed to having had 'some hair-breadth escapes from a well-scented pack of bloodhounds'. So where had he been holed up? By not sanctioning access, it was clear that Walker knew, and that he wasn't Brodie's only contact in London; that, despite having lived most of his life 500 miles away in Scotland, the fugitive was well enough connected down south to be accommodated by 'an old female friend who kept me snug and safe in her house within 500 yards of Bow Street' for ten days after his arrival.

Having been primed by a letter of introduction (and paid?) from north of the border by Brodie's cousin Milton, Mr Walker took very good care of Brodie too, lending him twelve guineas and arranging for him to be shipped out of London to the Continent, so being one of the 'some persons' referred to in the Lord Advocate's address – and abbreviated telling of the escape story – to the jury in the Deacon's trial:

I would, in the next place, gentlemen, have you to attend to the prisoner's behaviour when he flies from this place to London. He secretes himself in London for several weeks; search is made for him, but he cannot be found; he admits in one of his letters that he knew that Mr Williamson was in search of him, but he did not choose an interview; a vessel is freighted for him by some persons, contrary to the duty they owed to their country; she is cleared out for Leith; he goes on board of her in the middle of the night, with a wig on, in disguise, and under a borrowed name; he is carried to Flushing; he changes his name to John Dixon, and writes letters to people in Edinburgh under that false signature, explaining his whole future operations, in consequence of which letters he is traced and apprehended, just when he is on the point of going on board of a ship for New York. If he had been innocent ... it is not possible that he could have conducted himself in this manner.

The letters referred to, as well as passages given by witnesses in court, disclose much of the intriguing detail of Brodie's shipboard flight and so have been dealt with in separate chapters (5 and 6); only unelaborated stages of the voyage are recounted in this chapter, before looking at the dramatic circumstances of his flight, arrest and repatriation.

It was on yet another Sunday – 23 March – that Brodie found himself being led aboard the Scottish sloop *Endeavour*, of Carron near Falkirk, which lay at anchor at Blackwall and was supposedly set fair for Edinburgh's port of Leith with a couple of homeward-bound Scots passengers. It was just before midnight when the captain, John Dent, came aboard with the owners, Messrs Hamilton and Pinkerton, in the company of what looked like 'an elderly gentleman in feeble health' who was dressed in a blue great-coat with a pulled-up red collar, round wig, black vest, breeches and boots – and who – before the ship set off the next morning – 'was allotted a bed in the state room near the fire as he was sick'.

Another deep sigh of relief must have emanated from the state room that morning when the *Endeavour* came alive, her sails billowing out as her mooring ropes were loosened to allow her a good start with a fair wind into the broad Thames estuary. Brodie too must have relished the movement, comfortable in the knowledge – despite his chronically sore throat – that he was making good his escape, as only a clever fellow like him could do.

It was not to be quite so simple, however. Suddenly, just off Tilbury Point, the *Endeavour* made a heavy crunching noise as her hull scraped along the bottom of the sea; she had gone aground, and, despite the crew's energetic efforts to coax her out of trouble, she was not to be refloated to clear the Thames and get out to open sea for a fortnight.

In the resulting 'dead' time it became inevitable that the three Scots passengers would get to know each other. The others were John Geddes, a tobacconist in Mid-Calder, West Lothian, and his wife Margaret, who had been on a short break in London. As all three repeatedly paced the deck seeking fresh air amid waves of fog, there was much good-natured conversation, during which it became clear that the 'sick old man' who had come aboard in the darkness of their first day was relatively young and nimble of mind, despite the sore throat for which he had to go ashore at one point to buy some soothing milk. Turning on his legendary cheeky charm for the other passengers, he gave his name as John Dixon and, while volunteering little about his circumstances or professional interests, easily befriended the couple and at one point even took them ashore by skiff to a nearby village for dinner.

But when the *Endeavour* was finally refloated to resume her interrupted voyage, the Geddeses' original sailing plan was still not to be. To everyone else's surprise – including the captain's? – 'Mr Dixon' handed Dent sealed orders from the owners, in which he was instructed to change course from a direct path to Leith and make straight across the North Sea for Ostend, where 'Mr Dixon' was to be landed.

The couple's feeling about this could well be imagined, but they had little choice but to shrug off this further delay to their homeward voyage, and they would even then do 'Mr Dixon' a parting favour (that would ultimately backfire on him and have a serious effect on his future). As it happened, the weather was rough with cross winds, the ship failed to make Ostend and headed instead from Flanders to Flushing (Vlissingen) in The Netherlands.

What was that fateful favour? Having arrived at their unexpected destination on 8 April, the Geddeses were all set to say their farewells to 'Mr Dixon' – as he again boarded the skiff, to take him and his large trunk back to the ship's original destination of Ostend – when he handed them three letters with the request that they deliver them on their arrival in Edinburgh. These were addressed to his mistress Anne Grant, of Cant's Close; Michael Henderson, stabler in the Grassmarket; and his brother-in-law Matthew Sheriff, upholsterer in Edinburgh. The Geddeses warily agreed to do this as they waved their newfound friend goodbye.

But why were the letters so fateful? Simply because, not long after he got home, it became clear to John Geddes, on reading newspapers and listening to local gossip, that their friend was surely the sought-after Deacon Brodie; when, after three weeks of prevarication (was he wondering about related rewards?), he eventually turned the letters over to the authorities, in the shape of the sheriff, it was noted not only that he had already opened them but also that they gave fairly clear clues as to Brodie's likely whereabouts. So no more time would be lost in setting off to find him again.

By now, the Brodie hunt had become not just national – with many British ports on the look-out for him – but international, which threatened to thwart his plan to make his American getaway unnoticed from the other side of the North Sea. Details of his progress, locations and circumstances revealed by the letters were instantly despatched to the authorities in London, and the Secretary of State, Lord Carmarthen, at once contacted Sir John Potter, the British consul at Ostend, who in turn informally appointed a 'detective' with special knowledge of the case to set off in hot pursuit. He was one John Daly, an Irishman resident in Ostend, who knew that – after being in the town for about two months – Brodie had left Ostend and was on his way to Amsterdam.

This intelligence was based on Daly being a tenant of John Bacon, an English vintner in Ostend who met Brodie on 4 June when he came seeking company and advice, armed with a letter from the *Endeavour's* captain, which read:

Dear Friend

The bearer, John Dixon, was going passenger with me to New York but, being taken sick, had a desire to be landed at Ostend. Therefore, I recommend him to your care, being a countryman and a stranger; on my account, I hope you'll render him every service in your power. In so doing, you will oblige your most humble servant,

John Dent

The burly Irishman had not only seen the note but had also witnessed Bacon advising the Scottish visitor that, as there were plenty of ships leaving Amsterdam with goods, including weapons, to replenish America's post-Declaration of Independence skirmishes against the British, he would 'very easily' find a berth there to take him across the Atlantic.

It was when the authorities made some close-focused local enquiries that it became clear to both Bacon and Daly that the Scottish stranger they had been talking to was probably not John Dixon but the fugitive suspect William Brodie. It also became clear to them that there was a considerable reward payable on his arrest. Duly appointed, Daly, the amateur but enterprising 'detective', was soon on his way north in pursuit of Britain's most wanted man. It was mid-June and Brodie had probably already arrived in Amsterdam, but the tenacious Irishman was only about a week behind him and was determined to catch up.

★★★

Brodie's funds must have been fading fast. Before even reaching the Continent, and having paid for his sea passage with some of solicitor Walker's 'lent' twelve guineas, he had written: 'My stock is seven guineas, but when I reach Ostend will be reduced to less than six.' Somehow, he had found affordable digs for two months in Ostend and was now paying his way to Rotterdam, from where he would save money by taking the cheapest form of transport. The *trekschuit* horse-drawn canal sailboat was packed with goods and passengers like modern buses and, travelling at a horse-trotting speed of about 7km an hour, took many hours to cover what are today seen as short distances. In this case, the 84km trip from Rotterdam to Amsterdam took thirteen hours, with two hours spent crossing Delft on foot and changing again at Leidschendam, Leiden, Haarlem and Halfweg. At least it was faster than walking, and on his 10 June arrival, with his heavy trunk, at the (still-standing)

Haarlemmerpoort, the end-point of the network's service, Brodie was greeted by two Jews who had made it their business to guide new arrivals into town.

Where, he asked them, could he find a bed for a few nights? They directed him to an alehouse with lodgings, towards the harbour area but within walking distance, though he must have hired a cart to get his trunk there too. The pub's name was the Lommer (the Shadow) and it was crouched in an alleyway called Zoutsteeg just off the boat-busy central artery of the Damrak. Once he got there, made a deal with the landlord and heaved his trunk upstairs to his room on the first floor, with its pair of windows looking out into the lane, he must have thought he had made it, that he would be like the proverbial needle in a haystack for any pursuers now.

The last thing he expected within a few days of settling in was a hard, threatening knocking on the door of his 'impossible to find' refuge.

★★★

While being generally wary, Brodie probably had no suspicions that he had been followed. But within a few days Daly was in Amsterdam too, after linking up with the British ambassador in The Hague, Sir James Harris, to whom application for Brodie's arrest had been formally made. The Irishman quickly became acquainted with the two Jewish *trekschuit* receptionists who had helped the arriving Brodie, asking them if they could – in the name of the law – establish his whereabouts now. The Scot and his black trunk were described to them and recognised, and in return for a few loose coins, they walked the Irishman to the Lommer and left him there to complete his business.

When the landlord told him that the person he wished to speak to was in the room just above, Daly bounded upstairs – and that was when the knocking began.

Brodie froze, thought it wiser not to speak and so reveal his presence to his loud visitor, rolled quietly out of bed and tiptoed over to the room's only cupboard, secreting himself behind his own well-diminished collection of clothes ('My wardrobe is all on my back, excepting two check shirts and two white ones, one of them an old rag … my coat, an old blue one, out at the arms and elbows … an old striped waistcoat, and a pair of good boots'). He was surely mouse-quiet, but there must have been small bed-spring noises and door creaks that encouraged the door-knocker, for he hammered again and again, harder and harder – until deciding to let himself in. A quick glance around the room was all he needed before throwing open the cupboard door and revealing its cowering tenant.

'How do you do, Captain John Dixon alias William Brodie!' he boomed. 'I must ask you to come along with me.'

The no-longer-elusive Deacon, stunned into silence by this sudden development, considered making a fight of it. But despite having sported a pair of pistols in his darker career, he had never really been one for physical resistance or violence, and why would he start now in a metaphorical as well as a physical hands-up situation? Apart from which, he did not feel in the best of health.

So he went quietly, allowing himself a deep sigh of disappointment, and gathered together what clothes he could, before being hustled down the stairs past an astonished landlord.

If his fate had not been quite unredeemable before his desperate flight from Edinburgh, it certainly looked to be well and truly sealed here – 'looked' being the operative word, for the ever-clever William Brodie, still with an enigmatic smirk on the edge of his mouth, was never going to lose faith in his own ultimate survivability. Not even when they put a noose around his neck.

★★★

Does Brodie's alehouse refuge, de Lommer, still exist in Amsterdam? It appears not. There is no such pub now by that name in the Zoutsteeg, though a modern successor may occupy its building.

Someone from the 1780s would barely recognise the area today, however. The Damrak, from which the narrow alley runs at right angles, was a footpath-edged Venice-style major canal packed with wharves and a forest of the masts of light cargo-carrying vessels serving the city and its food processors and suppliers. The name Zoutsteeg itself – Salt Alley – gives an obvious clue to the trade that was carried on there, while other, parallel, lanes boast other give-away labels, such as Haringpakkersteeg (Herring Packers Alley). And it is certainly not quite so romantically picturesque today.

The major change came in 1875, when the Damrak was drained, filled in and covered over as a wide, traffic-carrying thoroughfare thrusting boldly between the Central Station (now fronting the old harbour) and Dam Square; so that today it is overflowing not just with cars, bikes, buses and clanging trams but with thousands of polyglot tourists thronging its wide pavements and staring in bewildered wonder at a positive kaleidoscope of souvenir shops, risqué museums, bureaux du change, hotels, Flemish patate frites vendors and even more souvenir shops selling everything from jolly painted clogs and brollies through sunglasses and baseball caps to orange football-themed T-shirts and phallic salt cellars – reminders that all this is only few hundred metres from the vastly more vivid vulgarity of the Red Light area a stone's throw behind the big street.

That said, its immediate opposite flank is a deal more sober, a brief island of sheer respectability dominated by the big square buildings of the Amsterdam Stock Exchange and the exclusive Bijenkorf department store that breathes Dutch prosperity (a fact of which this writer was made familiar when his son, preparing for a funeral, was delighted to acquire a black shirt in its 'sale' for a 'fantastically discounted' seventy euros).

From the Damrak, walking the Zoutsteeg's 100 paces to the busy parallel shopping street of Nieuwendijk and looking upwards to imagine which of the close-up buildings might have housed our legendary runaway, you see – among the side-by-side little shops selling *broodjes*, raw herring, tobacco and Chinese massages –

the remnants of an ancient chimney plaque with some barely legible lines which, if he had asked a local for a translation, might have alarmed Brodie. Its Dutch words 'De rook kan elk te kennen geven/De kortheid van het aardsche leven' mean in English 'From smoke we are to learn/The shortness of our earthly life'. The area's whole impact is circus-like – brash colours, loud street organs, ubiquitous tacky souvenirs – not unlike the tourist-attracting piped-up Royal Mile in Edinburgh.

It would have been reminiscent of Edinburgh, too, for William Brodie – for different reasons in his different age. Here then, too, were dark alleys between buildings like the Scottish capital's dark closes, and he could, under different circumstances, have felt comfortable in this vaguely familiar environment of his tavern lodging. As it was, he barely had time to avail himself of some of its other comforts and find a contact to identify a ship to take him to the New World – and his new life – when he heard that fateful first knock on his door.

★★★

There are today (as a matter of superficial opinion) three possible candidates for the relevant building that housed the Lommer and our fugitive in Zoutsteeg. One is a small, two-storey coffee shop called Kadinsky, at the far end of the alley, crowded on the ground floor with tightly packed clientele and a certain atmospheric pungency. Its timeless Dutch shape and relatively low physical standing tell of real age, as do the weather-beaten bricks of its walls. But while conceding that the upstairs office floor could have been a lodging room in times past, its female owner, on hearing the Brodie story, feels the place was probably too small to be a self-respecting criminal's refuge. 'If I'd been him,' she says with a smile, 'I'd have chosen a bigger place to get lost in.'

Another possibility is a bigger tavern, halfway up the lane, where the barman resists the urge to be fascinated, saying simply:

'This used to be a tobacconist.' But the best candidate is probably the Oporto, an old brown pub housed at the start of the alley in a taller, three-storey building of the bolder Golden Age type that has clearly enjoyed a relatively recent renovation. It also has a female proprietor, an Englishwoman called Fran, who says, 'As far as I know, the pub goes back to the 1880s but I suppose another inn could have been here under another name before that.'

Two regular customers are Scots house-painters keen to confirm their adopted pub's historic credentials after seeing evidence of some vintage with their own eyes. They recall doing décor work there during which they discovered, under a few more modern roof panels, some age-mottled wood marquetry of animals and plants. 'To us, that means this is sure to have been the place,' they say. Aye, maybe, as they say in their home town of Airdrie; Fran, meanwhile, says the pictures are from the pub's nineteenth-century inauguration, pointing out 'more like them' just behind the bar.

In the absence of utterly convincing evidence and the city archives' inability to help – despite the enhanced capacity of a newly installed computer system – the reader is invited to make a choice. In any case, Brodie didn't have much of a stay here, and it wasn't much of a walk to his next berth. Which was not, as he expected, aboard some fine big ship heading for that fast-growing American city that, until a century before, had been called New Amsterdam. It was a mere 260 steps away to the then the Stadhuis, or town hall (now the Royal Palace), at the head of Dam Square, where he was to be ensconced immediately in a cell below street level.

★★★

It is not hard to imagine Brodie's exchanges with Daly as they set out on that short, fateful and near-final stage of his continental journey. There would have been a familiarity about his new Irish companion and, as they paused briefly on leaving the pub, Brodie might have asked him: 'Have I not made your acquaintance somewhere?' After disclosing that he they had almost met a few days before before at the vintner's place in Ostend – and receiving a non-committal but thoughtful 'ah' – let's assume Daly removed his prisoner's cravat and wrapped it tightly around his wrists.

'Sorry, captain. Can't be too careful with a precious commodity like yourself. They tell me you can be a bit of slippery customer.'

'But how, pray, did you find me? I was unaware of a single soul following me.'

'I did not strictly follow on your tail, my friend, rather on your trail. Slippery snails leave a trail that glistens quite bright if they have no care to disguise it. I witnessed my landlord advising you to make haste for Amsterdam, and though you had a head start, I had merely to ask after you along the route.'

'Ugh, 'tis not a pretty picture you paint of me.'

'If I may venture to say so, sir, you have painted an ugly picture of yourself. But you would not deny, would you, that you are a singularly distinctive character? We Celts tend to be somewhat conspicuous in civilised society at any time. And especially so, I would suggest, when on the run from the powers of the law.'

'Indeed. I cannot deny it.'

'Well, if you ask me, you would be wise also not to deny the extent of your crimes.'

'Indeed, you may be right again, my friend. But where are you taking me?'

'You'll see.'

The rest of the short walk to Dam Square was probably taken in silence as the great, rectangular, multi-windowed Stadhuis building loomed up before them. And within minutes, Daly had shown his papers of authority and Brodie had been bundled away.

It is not recorded whether he was clapped in leg or wrist irons, but there would have been a good Dutch thoroughness about the definite turning – and further storage – of his cell key. He might have studied it with an experienced eye, but he would have realised there was no way he was going to unlock himself from this.

Having safely handed over his valuable captive, John Daly wasted no time in finding himself a ship to set out for British shores to claim his well-earned reward. So sure was he that there would be no need for further action in this now-concluded commission.

Perhaps not from him, but other relevant actions were being frantically undertaken. The Amsterdam Archives of Sheriffs and Magistrates record the following (as translated from the old Dutch):

On the 25th of June 1788 Mr Henry Pye Rich, Consul & Agent of His Royal Majesty of Great Britain, gave the Head Officer a written request with the following content: The undersigned… requests immediately that the person of William Brodie, accused of committing a flagrant and important robbery in Edinburgh, Scotland, be held securely in custody at the cost of … [signed] Henry Pye Rich.

The archives also guaranteed 'detective' Daly his place in history by stating that 'the named William Brodie was apprehended by a certain John Daly of Ostend in a house called de Lommer in the Zoutsteeg, and was taken from there to De Boeijen [the prison cells in the basement of the town hall]'. But most importantly, the archives have on record the official request of the British to the Dutch for 'possession' of Brodie. Kindly translated for this book by Dutch writer Marco Daane – a long-interested researcher of the case – it goes like this, with the warning from him that 'of course it is in an anachronistic kind of language with lots of angles and curves in the sentences':

The noble and honourable justice of the Town of Amsterdam, upon request by me, Henry Pye Rich, consul & agent for His Majesty the King of Great Britain, have been so good as to apprehend and hand over to me to be transported to England, one William Brodie.

Therefore, in my aforementioned quality, I herewith declare that this transfer will not be used to damage the Justice of Amsterdam, not by me nor by anyone else, and so in consequence to the disadvantage or reduction of the rights, authority and jurisdiction of the aforementioned Town, and also that I will not indicate this act in any different way than as a matter of service to Justice, for which I am prepared to declare it is excused, while I also accept to reimburse any costs that have been made after they were declared.

[signed] Henry Pye Rich,

Amsterdam, 8 July, 1788

But before releasing the prisoner to the British authorities, the Dutch had to be absolutely sure he was who he was said to be.

★★★

Meanwhile, one John Groves, a public officer clerk of London's famous crime-fighting Bow Street, had been also on the miscreant's trail, only to be beaten to the prize by the Irishman; yet he was still expected to take charge of the prisoner and bring him back to face his fate in his own country. How had Groves become involved? That was later explained at Brodie's trial, when London solicitor Thomas Longlands was sworn in as a prosecution witness and asked to recall his role in the case. He was asked: 'Did you hear of William Brodie, the prisoner at the bar, having fled from this country in March last, and of his having been brought back? Tell the court what you know of the matter.'

He replied:

In the month of June or July last I was employed by the officers of the Crown for Scotland to take such steps as appeared to me to be proper for the discovery of Mr Brodie. In consequence of this employment I called frequently at the Secretary of State's Office, and had several conversations with Mr Fraser, Under-Secretary in the office of Lord Carmarthen, and gave them the information I had received from Scotland.

I likewise waited upon Sir Sampson Wright, of the Public Office, Bow Street, whose assistance I judged necessary to call in as to the proper measures to be pursued. As the information received gave reason to suspect that Mr Brodie was at Flushing, Ostend, or some place in Holland, it was agreed upon to send a messenger immediately in search of him. Sir Sampson Wright recommended to me a Mr Groves from his office as a proper person to send to the Continent in search of Mr Brodie, and I accordingly despatched him with proper instructions.

Mr Groves traced Mr Brodie to Ostend, and learned that he had been there upon the 4th of June, His Majesty's birthday, and he was afterwards traced to Amsterdam, where he was apprehended, identified, and committed to prison. Upon proper application, he was delivered up to Mr Groves, and was brought from thence to London by him.

What follows is Groves' account of his 'expedition-and-extradition' experience in his own words, taken from his journal:

On Tuesday, the 1st July, I left London, and arrived at Harwich at three o'clock the next morning.

Wednesday, waited on Mr Coxe, the agent for the packet, with Mr [William] Fraser's letter, and also on the Captain, who dined with me. At half-past four in the afternoon sailed out of the harbour, and lost sight of land at nine.

Thursday, got sight of Helvoetsluys [the principal port for the English packets from Harwich] at twelve next day, – dead calm four leagues from shore, – rowed into the harbour in the long boat, with Captain Hearne, and Carpmeal, (Sir S. Wright's officer), with the mail, and a woman going as Lady's maid to Sir James Harris's Lady, – drove back by tide, and almost out to sea again, – landed on sand, walked to several farmhouses, leaving the mail and baggage on the sand, guarded, in quest or a waggon, – refused; – a boor, at last, went at an extravagant price; we had walked seven miles on hot sands, and parched with thirst; at eight o'clock waggon came with the mail, &c. – set out for the Brill, but, within two miles, waggon

broke down, and obliged to procure boors to carry mail, &c. arrived
at the Brill at half past nine; – Brooks, the messenger, came from
Helvoetsluys to meet us, where he had been waiting, — had heard
nothing of any person (Englishman) being in custody at Amsterdam,
which much alarmed me, nor had Hutchinson, the collector of the
passports, – more alarmed; – delivered Mr Fraser's letter to Brooks; –
at ten set off with Brooks for Maslinsluys, arrived there at half-past
eleven, got to Delft at three-quarters past twelve; – arrived at the
Hague at three in the morning in an open post waggon, with heavy
rain, thunder and lightning.

Friday, waited on Sir James Harris [British ambassador in
The Hague] at ten in the morning, – introduced to Brooks, – treated
with great affability, and received a letter from Sir James, which he
had already wrote, directed to Mr Henry Rich [British consul in
Amsterdam]. Sir James having first informed me that Brodie was
safe in the Stadthouse, – consulted Sir James on the mode of obtain-
ing him, – informed that, if the magistrates of Amsterdam required
an official application to the States General, to come back immediately to him, and he would obviate all difficulties; but he did not
think it would be necessary: – it was Sir James's opinion the magistrates would give him up without, if not, was certain they would
detain him till an answer to Sir James's application to the States
could be obtained; – set off for Amsterdam, and arrived there the
same evening; waited on Mr Rich, – politely received; and we consulted on measures, – Mr Rich to wait on one of the magistrates
that evening, and to send to me early next morning. – Waited on
Mr Duncan, a Scots gentleman, and father-in-law to Mr Gerard,
a minister at Amsterdam, with Mr Longlands's letter; – Mr Duncan
seemed willing to identify Brodie; but on being called out into
another room by Mr Gerard and his wife, on his return, Mr D. said,
as far as his word of honour as a gentleman would go, and his belief,
he would say he was the man; but, if an oath was required he would
not. – Saw then a manifest reluctance in Mr D. and had no doubt
his daughter and the parson would endeavour to persuade him to

decline troubling himself in the matter; but judged he could not go back from what he had said to Mr Rich.

N.B. No mischief but a woman or a priest in it, – here both.

Saturday morning, received a message from Mr Rich, – most of the magistrates gone to their country-houses, – nothing could be done till Monday; – Mr Rich entertained no doubt, but said a magistrate had informed him, that a formal requisition must be made by him, in writing, to the magistrates; – he produced the copy of one, requiring the person of William Brodie to be delivered up; I corrected it, by inserting 'otherwise John Dixon', as the magistrates of Amsterdam knew of no William Brodie; Mr Rich agreed it was proper; – informed him of my suspicions respecting Mr Duncan, and the steps that would be taken by his family to make him, if possible, recant; – my fears further increased, as Mr Duncan lodged in the same tavern with me, I had frequent opportunities of conversation with him, and could plainly see a sorrow for what he had said, and a wish to retract.

Monday, waited on Mr Rich, – found, by a mistake in not inserting 'otherwise John Dixon' in the requisition, that the business must be delayed till the next day ten o'clock, when a general meeting of the magistrates, with the grand schout (high sheriff) to consider on the application; – mistake corrected, and requisition presented.

Tuesday, sent for by the magistrates to the Stadthouse; – from their manner, judged Brodie's delivery as predetermined; – Mr Duncan sent for.

Predetermined perhaps, but not so simple to execute. As it happened, while everyone involved in the case knew who the prisoner was, some difficulty was encountered in formally establishing his identity, and John Groves – sometimes referring to himself in the third person – reported further on the challenge of getting sworn witnesses (preferred by Dutch law) at the showdown meeting between Brodie and the Amsterdam magistrates questioning him. The attitude of the aforementioned Mr Duncan proved frustrating for the meeting. Why? He said he was not a native of Edinburgh but of Aberdeen, that he frequently visited Edinburgh on business and that eight, ten or twelve years before – he couldn't say which – the man now calling himself John Dixon was pointed out to him as Deacon Brodie. He had seen him several times after that and always understood him to be Deacon Brodie, though he did not know his Christian name. He had no doubt this was the same man, but 'he would not swear he had no doubt – a nice distinction'.

Brodie was ordered to be brought in and, as he faced the magistrates with an unusually downtrodden expression, he seemed nonetheless also determined to err seriously on the side of caution, being prepared to admit nothing.

Here is Grove's reporting of the High Sheriff's relevant exchange with the prisoner, who was first asked the following:

What is your name?

John Dixon.

That is the name you go by here – but is not your real name William Brodie?

My Lords, I stand here and claim the protection of the laws of this country, which require two witnesses, on oath, to prove me William Brodie.

You shall have the protection of the laws of this country, but they do not require two oaths to identify you; it requires that the magistrates shall be satisfied you are the same man.

Mr Groves – I beg leave he may be asked, if he is not a native of Edinburgh?

Question put – the answer, *I have been at Edinburgh.*

Mr Groves – Is he a Deacon of Edinburgh?

Prisoner replied – *I claim the protection of the laws.*

Mr Groves – Does he know Mr William Walker, Attorney at law, of the Adelphi, London?

Prisoner replied – *I know such a man.*

Mr Groves – Then that William Walker procured the escape of this William Brodie from London, which I can prove by extracts of letters now in my pocket, the originals of which are here in the hands of your officers. I can swear to Mr Walker's writing.

Here the Magistrates asked me [Groves] if I was ready to swear that, from the pointed description of him and all said circumstances, he was, to the best of my belief, the man required to be given up? – I told them I was.

Mr Duncan was then asked if, from what he knew and what he had heard, he would swear he had no doubt, and believed him to be the man.

Mr Duncan's reply – *I am only a visitor here; and being called on such an occasion, it might, in my own country where I am a Magistrate, have the appearance of forwardness if I was to swear. I am a man of honour and a gentleman, and my word ought to be taken. I do believe, and I have no doubt, that he is the same man; but I decline to swear it; I'll take no oath.*

The Magistrates expostulated, but unsuccessfully, on the absurd idea of saying, 'I have no manner of doubt, and verily believe' and refusing to swear (that) 'I have no manner of doubt'.

As I had previously drawn up an information for Mr Duncan and myself to that effect, he was asked if he would sign it without swearing? – Mr Duncan said he would.

The Magistrates then said that they should pay the same compliment to me they did to Mr Duncan, and take my signature to the certificate, without an oath, even to my belief. – [Certificate signed].

The prisoner was then ordered in, and the certificate read to him, and asked if he had not a father? – He replied, *None.*

But you had a father, said the Judge – was not his name Brodie?

Prisoner replied – *There are more Brodies than one.*

Then by that, said the Judge, you confess your name is Brodie?

A lapsus linguae, my Lord.

It was, indeed, a sensational lapse, or slip of the tongue. Realising that he had blundered like a mouse into a clever legal eagle's claws, Brodie tried desperately to struggle out by again stressing what he believed was a technical requirement for witnesses' oaths. But the judge told him bluntly that the matter was closed; that all they wanted was to be satisfied about his identity, which they now were from what had been signed by Mr Duncan and Mr Groves, and partly from that virtual confession of his own. It was time to go home, the captured fugitive was told. He was duly marked for delivery to Mr Groves, who was advised by the judge that he should have a guide and waste no time in setting off that day.

As it happened, when the journey-ready Bow Street clerk returned to the Stadhuis to get going with Brodie at 4 p.m., there were no fewer than four guides waiting for him, not to mention eight horses pulling two carriages, into one of which the 'properly secured' Brodie was sharply bundled. A 'prodigious crowd' had gathered to watch them leave like some kind of royal party and, had he had his hands free, no doubt the Deacon would have waved regally to them like some kind of royal personage. It's not hard to imagine that, despite his recent refugee status, the self-regarding little man would have resented the severe lack of dignity he was now suffering. And it was to get worse even after they arrived at Helvoetsluys around lunchtime the next day. Here the packet had been waiting for them after Groves had written to Sir James Harris on the Saturday requesting that it be detained – 'who informed me by Mr Rich, with whom I dined on the Monday, that it should be detained to the last moment'.

When they sailed for Harwich, the erstwhile Mr John Dixon was 'watched two hours alternately on board by the ship's crew, his hands and arms confined, and his meat cut up for him, &c' and must have registered some regret that he was not enjoying the comforts of his earlier voyage, not to mention the much greater regret he felt about not managing to follow through his major life plan.

Groves ended his story by saying, 'On Thursday night, eleven o'clock, we arrived at Harwich – supped – set off immediately, and arrived next day at noon at Sir Sampson Wright's, before whom, and Mr Longlands, Brodie confessed he was the person advertised.'

The said Thomas Longlands, a London solicitor employed by the Crown officers of Scotland for this case, took up the next part of the tale when he appeared as a witness at the Deacon's trial (page 146). He said that, immediately on arrival in London from the Netherlands, and before being sent back to Scotland, Brodie was 'examined' along with two trunks belonging to him. They contained items whose provenance was obviously suspect, and Longlands – who was present – discovered 'a wrapper with some papers' in one which 'made a great impression on me at the time'.

It was at this point that George Williamson, the king's messenger who had searched for Brodie in vain before he sailed off from London, made a re-appearance – having been sent from Edinburgh to accompany the prisoner back to his home town. In the post chaise driving north, with Mr Groves also on board, Brodie seemed to relish the idea of the robber surprising and entertaining his captors. He soon demonstrated that, despite suffering apparent depression, he had lost none of his sense of mischief, and though they were now most definitely on opposite sides of society's fence, they seemed to enjoy each other's company, as Williamson later wrote: 'Mr Brodie was in good spirits, and told of many things that had happened to him in Holland.'

What kind of things? Williamson would not have been prepared to put some of them down on record, but one story concerned a friendship that Brodie had struck up with a fellow Scot (and fellow criminal) during his short stay among the canals. This man claimed to be a master-forger and was living in the city by means of presenting home-made Bank of Scotland notes where he could. This had clearly intrigued Brodie, who would certainly have wished to become such an expert in a black art that he seemed to have missed out on in his second career. Indeed, he was already receiving early instruction from this expert practitioner when his studies were abruptly halted by Mr Daly's call.

'Brodie said he was a very ingenious fellow, and that, had it not been for his own apprehension, he would have been master of the process in a week', wrote Williamson later.

There were a few shared chortles too when Brodie recalled his heavily escorted journey from Amsterdam's town house to his Delta port of departure. With a twinkle in his eyes, he talked of how one of his guides sported a beautiful gold watch and of how, if he had been so inclined, he could have easily relieved the 'well-oiled' owner of the treasure – and now regretted not doing so.

Such an accessory would doubtless have made his re-entrance into Edinburgh even more gasp-inducing than his usual personal style, which he was determined to restore – if only temporarily – before finding himself in a cage again. To that end, he persuaded Wiliamson to allow him a close shave, as he had been – up till Mr Daly's intervention – quite a master of the close shave. Williamson, alert to all possibilities of an open razor in the hands of a doomed criminal in the cabin of a bouncing coach, refused to let him perform the task – but offered to do it himself.

The Deacon, as one so good with his hands, was not entirely in admiration of his escort's 'barbarous' efforts and, when the operation was over, commented: 'George, if you're no better at your own business than at shaving, a person may employ you once, but I'll be damned if ever he does so again!'

They arrived in Edinburgh on 17 July after 'only' fifty-four hours on the road, noted the *Caledonian Mercury* as it reported:

> This morning early Mr Brodie arrived from London. He was immediately carried to the house of Mr Sheriff Archibald Cockburn [His Majesty's Sheriff-depute of the sheriffdom of Edinburgh], at the back of the Meadows, or Hope Park, for examination. Mr George Williamson, Messenger, and Mr Groves, one of Sir Sampson Wright's clerks, accompanied Mr Brodie in a post-chaise from Tothilfields Bridewell. He was this forenoon committed to the Tolbooth.

At the Tolbooth prison in the city's High Street, only about 100 yards from his erstwhile home and workshop, he made the following declaration to Sheriff Cockburn:

That he does not at present recollect the name of the vessel in which the declarant went from the river Thames to Holland in the month of April last; that is, in which he arrived at Holland in April last.

That, before he left the vessel, he gave some letters, at present he does not recollect the number, written by himself, to one Geddes, a passenger on board the vessel.

And being shown a letter directed to Michael Henderson, signed W.B., dated Thursday, the 10th of April last, declares that he cannot say that the letter was not wrote by him and given to Geddes.

And, being interrogated, if one of the letters given to Geddes was not directed to Mr Matthew Sheriff, upholsterer in Edinburgh, and signed John Dixon, dated Flushing, Tuesday, the 8th of April, 1788? – Declares that the declarant cannot give any positive answer to that question, and he does not suppose he would have signed any letter at that time by the name of John Dixon, especially as he had wrote some letters at the same time, and given them to Geddes, signed by his initials W. B.

Declares that the declarant, when taken into custody at Amsterdam, on the 26th of June last, went by the name of John Dixon.

Declares that the declarant first became acquainted with George Smith in Michael Henderson's a long while ago, when Smith was indisposed and bedfast there; that the declarant has been in George Smith's house in the Cowgate. And being interrogated, declares that he cannot say positively whether he was in Smith's house any day of the week before the declarant left Edinburgh, which, to the best of the declarant's recollection, he did upon the 9th of March last, and upon a Sunday, as he thinks.

Declares that, having received a message that some person in the jail of Edinburgh wanted to see him, he went there and found it was either Smith or Ainslie who had been inquiring for him; but the declarant, when going there, was told by the keeper that neither Smith nor Ainslie could be seen; and that this was the night preceding his departure from Edinburgh.

Being interrogated, If reports had not been going of the Excise Office having been broke into the week before the declarant left Edinburgh, if he, the declarant, would have taken that step? – declares that it was not in consequence of that report that he left Edinburgh, but that the declarant, being acquainted with Smith and Ainslie, then in custody, did not know what they might be induced to say to his prejudice, was the cause of his going away.

A mischievous thought to share with readers on leaving this chapter: looking around central Amsterdam on the Brodie trail, this writer noticed that the entrance to the Royal Palace on Dam Square (once the Stadhuis where Brodie was held after arrest) was 'guarded' by four ornate, cast-iron lampposts, each bearing the inscription 'Dixon, Amsterdam, 1844'. Though the designer was Tetar van Elven, the Dixon founder's credit prompted a double take – and, considering there could never have been many folk of that English name in Holland, some fantasising as to what might have lain behind what looks like a tribute to someone called Dixon, from someone else called Dixon.

A son, perhaps? Just imagine the last few nights of fugitive Brodie in a lonely room in Amsterdam, within easy walking distance of the Red Light area. Would he have been tempted to strike up a 'professional' relationship with one of the city's famous working girls? Did she come back to his room? Did he give her his 'safe' name (John Dixon)? Might she have become pregnant and given the resulting son his father's surname? And might that son have grown up to learn the story of his father's incarceration at what was by then the country's most conspicuous royal palace? Was he the proprietor of an iron foundry? He would have been 58 at the time.

In the time-honoured manner of journalists not wishing to spoil a good story by seeking out too many facts, we confess to not entirely pursuing this inventive thought – to not checking it at all, actually. So should any member of the Amsterdam Dixon family rise up in protest at such an outrageous suggestion, pre-emptive profuse apologies are herewith extended. In any case, the lampposts were cleaned and painted rich green in 1997 and are well worth a second look.

5

THE LAST LETTERS
OF HIS LIFE

No doubt about it, William Brodie was good with his hands. With no small thanks to his father's teachings, he could guide a plane and bevel an edge with a true artisan's skills, and even when fleeing the country could write a concerned letter asking after 'my quadrant and spirit level … my brass-cased measuring line, and three-foot rule'. And in the very writing of such a letter there was a clear manual dexterity, if not an artistic bent, in the fluent flow of his copperplate handwriting – which is still to be seen in existing letters such as his last-minute plea to the Duchess of Buccleuch to use her influence in having his death sentence changed to transportation to Botany Bay, where 'in that Infant Collony I might be usefull, from my knowledge in severall Mechanical branches besides my own particular Profession' (see chapter 7). Also in his letters there was a certain erudition to be seen, as well as the occasional classical turn of phrase that obviously sprang from his expensive Edinburgh education.

Pen and ink were therefore essential travelling companions for him, even while being pursued across the North Sea. He clearly needed to write – about his mindset and predicament and concerns for his various families, whether illegitimate children or fighting cocks – and in looking back at the last letters of his life, penned aboard his escape ship or in his death-row cell in the Tollbooth prison, we get a fairly clear picture of the delusions and denials of a self-destroyed man trying to hang on to the last threads of normalcy.

Three of those missives – written mainly at sea – found their way back to Scotland through the cautious kindness of the afore-mentioned fellow-traveller John Geddes of Mid-Calder, who eventually released them to the authorities. However, he did not do so without some prevarication, doubt and a growing curiosity about them which eventually – on discovering that the letter-writer and shipmate he had known as John Dixon was in fact Deacon Brodie – led to the frowned-upon opening of the letters.

This was recalled during Brodie's trial, where the tobacconist's wife, Margaret, set the shipboard scene:

> I was in London with my husband in March last, and went with him on board of a vessel bound for Leith. One night, when it was dark, a person, whom I now see a prisoner at the bar, and some others with him, came on board. The prisoner remained on board, but the others went ashore in about half-an-hour afterwards.
>
> I think the person had a wig on when he came on board, and he appeared to be in bad health. He passed by the name of John Dixon. The vessel sailed for the coast of Holland, and when she arrived there the prisoner went on shore. I saw my husband receive a packet of letters from Mr Dixon; but I know nothing more of them. I never saw these letters afterwards.

Not so her husband, who was first asked by Solicitor-General Robert Dundas: 'Do you know the prisoner ... would you know that person again?'

Geddes replied: 'I would.'

Dundas continued, 'Look at the prisoners at the bar and say if you know either of them.' (Here Geddes identified Brodie as the man who called himself John Dixon aboard ship.)

Geddes continued:

On getting out to sea Mr Dixon delivered to the captain a letter from [ship owners] Mr Hamilton or Mr Pinkerton, but, although I desired him to let me read it, I did not see it. In consequence of this, the captain altered his course and steered for Holland, and the vessel, although bound for Leith, sailed to Flushing. I do not think she was driven there by contrary winds, as the wind was south-west, and fairer for Newcastle or Leith than for Holland.

During the voyage, Mr Dixon complained much of a sore throat. When we arrived at Flushing we cleaned ourselves and went ashore, and Mr Dixon set off for Ostend in a skiff which he hired for that purpose. On shore, before he left, Mr Dixon gave me a packet containing two letters, one of which had another within it, to carry to Scotland to be delivered in Edinburgh. One of the letters was directed to Mr Michael Henderson, stabler in the Grassmarket, in which there was one inclosed to Mrs Anne Grant, Cant's Close, and the other to Mr Matthew Sheriff, upholsterer in Edinburgh, signed and dated as mentioned in the indictment.

We did no business at Flushing, and I am of opinion that the ship did not come there with that intention. After landing Mr Dixon we sailed for Leith. When I arrived in Leith, from the accounts I heard about Brodie, I was convinced that Dixon and Brodie were the same person. Next day I went to Mid-Calder, and about three weeks afterwards was at Dalkeith, where I had occasion to see the newspapers, and the description of Brodie therein given confirmed me in the above suspicion. I then delivered the letters to Sheriff Cockburn. I had previously opened the packet and read them. [*The letters were shown to Geddes at this point*]. I know that these are the letters I received from the prisoner and delivered to the Sheriff.

The Dean of Faculty Henry Erskine asked, 'Pray, sir, when did you open these letters you have told us of? Was it before or after you came to Leith?' – and there were many more questions:

Geddes – 'It was after.'

Erskine – 'You told us, sir, that upon reading the newspapers you discovered that Dixon and Brodie were one and the same person. Pray, sir, when or where did you first read the newspapers?'

Geddes – 'At Dalkeith.'

Erskine – 'How long was that after your arrival?'

Geddes – 'Three weeks.'

Erskine – 'And pray, sir, what was the reason that in all that time you did not deliver these letters to the persons to whom they were directed?'

Geddes – 'I did not remember that I had such letters when I was in Edinburgh myself, and I afterwards wished my brother-in-law to deliver them.'

Erskine – 'Did you open the letters?'

Geddes – 'I did.'

Erskine – 'And what was your reason for doing so?'

Geddes – 'I opened them and delivered them to the Sheriff for the good of my country.'

Erskine – 'And would it not have been as much for the good of the country to have delivered them without opening them?'

Geddes – 'I just opened them, and that's all; I can give no other reason.'

Erskine – 'Did you inform any person that you had such letters?'

Geddes – 'I did. I informed John Tweddle, my brother-in-law, who advised me to deliver them to the persons for whom they were intended. I afterwards showed them to a gentleman named Mr Learmonth in Linlithgow, who wrote a letter by me to a gentleman of this place. By him I was carried to Mr Erskine, but he would give me no advice, and therefore I returned home to Mid-Calder. That same evening, or early next morning, Mr Scott, Procurator-Fiscal, and Mr Williamson, messenger, called upon me, and I accompanied them to Edinburgh and delivered the letters to the Sheriff.'

Erskine – 'My Lords, as Mr Geddes has mentioned his having called upon me, I beg leave to state to the Court what passed upon the occasion. He was brought to my house by a gentleman, and he showed me the letters. I informed him that I was counsel for Mr Brodie; that he himself knew best the directions that he had received from the person who committed these letters to his charge; and that I could give him no other advice than this, that he ought to do in the matter that which his own conscience should point out to him as most proper.'

The judge, Lord Braxfield, then commented: 'That was a very proper advice, and was just what I would have expected from Henry Erskine.'

So what did they say? While the letters written during Brodie's seaborne getaway had taken on a certain curiosity value and provided something of a window into his state of mind, their importance in reinforcing his alleged guilt was not immediately apparent – until it was noted that one of them seemed to contain a slipped-out implicit admission of involvement in one of the gang's 'depredations'.

Not unexpectedly then, Brodie himself was keen to minimise their significance by feigning memory lapses in their regard. In his declaration reported by Archibald Cockburn, sheriff-depute of the shire of Edinburgh, he admits:

Before he [Brodie] left the vessel, he gave some letters, at present he does not recollect the number, written by himself, to one Geddes, a passenger on board ... And being shown a letter directed to Michael Henderson, signed W. B., dated Thursday, the 10th of April last, declares that he cannot say that the letter was not wrote by him and given to Geddes. And, being interrogated, if one of the letters given to Geddes was not directed to Mr Matthew Sheriff, upholsterer in Edinburgh, and signed John Dixon, dated Flushing, Tuesday, the 8th of April, 1788? – [he] cannot give any positive answer to that question, and he does not suppose he would have signed any letter at that time by the name of John Dixon, especially as he had wrote some letters at the same time, and given them to Geddes, signed by his initials W.B.

'And, being shown … another, dated Thursday, 10th April, 1788, directed to Mrs. Anne Grant, Cant's Close, Edinburgh, signed W. B., and, desired to say whether or not the said three letters are holograph of the declarant? – declares he does not incline to give any positive answer, the appearance of writing varies so much. This he declares to be truth.

Reproduced on the following pages are two of the three letters from his shipboard adventure – the one addressed to Anne Grant was deemed by the court 'too personal' to publish – as well as several 'scrolls' (tantalisingly unaddressed and oddly signed) originating from his trunk after his arrest in Amsterdam. There are also notes from his prison cell, where he was afforded the rare luxury of a desk and writing facilities.

Among the cast of names referred to in the letters are his two mistresses, the aforementioned Anne Grant and Jean Watt; George Williamson, the king's messenger for Scotland who initially pursued him in vain for eighteen days; Sir James Harris, British ambassador in The Hague; Mr Rich, British consul in Amsterdam; Sir Sampson Wright, chief magistrate at Bow Street, London; Robert Smith, Brodie's foreman; Mr Learmonth, adviser to the Geddes couple; William Martin, bookseller and auctioneer who was to buy and sell a property of Brodie's for his creditors; the Rev Nairn, who facilitated his getaway from Edinburgh and would help brother-in-law Mathew Sheriff organise the fugitive's finances; and Brodie's cousin Milton, supplier of moral support and an introduction to William Walker, attorney in the Adelphi, London, who busied himself in the fugitive's affairs, lent him twelve guineas and arranged for his passage to the Continent as soon as the coast was thought to be clear.

Of Sartorial Concerns

The earliest letter from the ship's destination of Flushing – or Vlissingen, to use its Dutch name, or the port of Helvoetsluys, to be precise – was addressed to Edinburgh upholsterer Matthew Sheriff, Brodie's brother in-law as husband of his sister Jacobina. It stressed the fugitive's regret, among several other loose-end concerns, at now being unable to dress to his normal high standards and his consequent requirement for 'liberal remittances', presumably to relieve this and other inconveniences. It was apparently the first (and last?) time Brodie had signed off a letter with his briefly adopted name of John Dixon, and it revealed that, under that name, he had been planning to head for New York, where – hopefully – money and goods requested of his contacts would be awaiting him, ready to help him start his new life.

Flushing, Tuesday, 8th April, 1788,
12 o'clock forenoon.

My dear Friend,

Sunday, the 23rd ult., I went on board a ship cleared out for Leith, but by a private bargain with the captain was to be landed at Ostend. I have been on board ever since the 23rd. Most of the time we lay aground a little below Gravesend. Owing to thick weather and cross wind, we are obliged to land here; but this afternoon I will set off, by water, for Bruges, and then for Ostend (so I begin my travels where most gentlemen leave them off), where I shall remain, for some time at least, until I hear from Mr Walker; and, indeed, I will require three weeks to recruit, for I have suffered more from my sore throat than sufficient to depress the spirits of most men.

There was for twenty days I did not eat ten ounces of solid meat; but, thank God, I am now in a fair way. My stock is seven guineas, but by I reach to Ostend will be reduced to less than six. My wardrobe is all on my back, excepting two check shirts and two white ones, one of them an old rag I had from my cousin Milton, with an old hat (which I left behind), my coat, an old blue one, out at the arms and elbows, I also had from him, with an old striped waistcoat, and a pair of good boots. Perhaps my cousin judged right, that old things were best for my purpose. However, no reflections; he is my cousin, and a good prudent lad, and showed great anxiety for my safety; rather too anxious, for he would not let me take my black coat with me, nor Mr Nairn's great-coat, which makes me the worse off at present; but I could not extract one guinea from him, although he owes me twenty-four pounds for three years past.

He turned me over to Mr Walker, who supplied me with twelve guineas. He is a gentleman I owe much to. I wish I may ever have it in my power to show my gratitude to him and Mr Nairn. Had Milton been in my place, and me in his, my purse, my credit, and my wardrobe, my all, should have been at his disposal. However, let not this go farther, lest it should have an appearance of reflection upon a worthy man. He cannot help his natural temper.

I would have wrote to Mr Nairn, but for certain reasons I believe it is not proper at present. Please to communicate this to him. And I beg that everything may be sent to me that you, Mr Nairn, and my sisters may think useful to me, either in wearing apparel, tools, or even a small assortment of brass and iron work. Please send my quadrant and spirit level; they lie in a triangular box in my old bedroom. My brass-cased measuring line, and three-foot rule, my silver stock buckle, it is in the locker of my chest, and my stocks, they will save my neckcloths. If my sister pleases to send me some hand towels, they will be serviceable to me, whether I keep a house or a room.

I most earnestly beg of Mr Nairn that my remittances be as liberal as possible; for without money I can make but a poor shift; for, you must think, my days for hard labour is near expiring, although, with my constitution, I may be able to carry on business for many years, and perhaps with success.

I have not yet received the trunk with my shirts and stockings, but will write Mr Walker to forward it to Ostend, where I will be under the necessity of buying some things. And I hope by the time I come to New York I will have some things waiting me there. Whether it is best to send them by the Clyde or Thames, you and Mr Nairn will judge best. And I hope to have a long letter from each of you, and one from my sister Jeany; and your's will include your wife's. They may be put in with my things,

and any other letters my friends are pleased to send. Direct for Mr John
Dixon, to the care of the Revd. Mr Mason, at New York. I am not sure of
settling there, but will make for it as soon as I can.

    I have no more time, the boat just going off for Bruges or Ostend.

I am,

Dear Sir,

Yours for ever,

John Dixon.

On the back of this sheet he had written: 'Let my name and destination be a profound secret, for fear of bad consequences.'

The Uneasy Father

The following is a two-part letter, signed W.B., to his constant
friend Michael Henderson, owner of the Grassmarket stables where
fighting cocks (including those bred and entered by Brodie) had
made many a man bankrupt as they were set against each other in
a noisy pit of blood, flying feathers and death. The faraway Brodie
was clearly still excited by the spectacle and not yet so concerned
with his own plight as to forget that one of his birds was recently in
action – and he enquires here as to how it fared. He also asks about
the welfare of his various children, and to see this man of many
conflicting parts as a deeply 'uneasy' father is to see him in yet
another light. The letter also reveals that, while George Williamson
failed to catch sight of him on their near-parallel travels, Brodie had
seen his pursuer 'twice' but had not, of course, introduced himself.

Thursday, 10th April, 1788.

Dear Michael,

    I embrace this opportunity of writing you, and I make no doubt but it
will give you, Mrs. Henderson, and a few others satisfaction to hear that
I am well.

Were I to write you all that has happened to me, and the hairbreadth escapes I made from a well-scented pack of bloodhounds, it would make a small volume.

I left Edinburgh Sunday, the 9th, and arrived in London Wednesday, the 12th, where I remained snug and safe in the house of an old female friend until Sunday, 23rd March (whose care for me I shall never forget, and only wish I may ever have it in my power to reward her sufficiently), within 500 yards of Bow Street. I did not keep the house all this time, but so altered, excepting the scar under my eye, I think you could not have rapt [swore] to me. I saw Mr Williamson twice; but, although countrymen commonly shake hands when they meet from home, yet I did not choose to make so free with him, notwithstanding he brought a letter to me; he is a clever man, and I give him credit for his conduct.

My female gave me great uneasiness by introducing a flash man to me, but she assured me he was a true man, and he proved himself so, notwithstanding the great reward, and was useful to me. I saw my picture [his description in a newspaper] six hours before exhibited to public view, and my intelligence of what was doing at Bow Street Office was as good as ever I had in Edinburgh. I left London on Sunday, 23rd March, and from that day to this present moment, that I am now writing, have lived on board a ship, which life agrees vastly well with me. It is impossible for me at present to give you my address, but I beg you will write me, or dictate a letter to Thom, and let it be a very long one, giving me an account of what is likely to become of poor Ainslie, Smith, and his wife; I hope that neither you, nor any of your connections, has been innocently involved by those unfortunate men, or by that designing villain Brown; I make no doubt but he is now in high favour with [sheriff-depute] Mr Cockburn, for I can see some strokes of his pencil in my portrait. May God forgive him for all his crimes and falsehoods.

I hope in a short time to be in Edinburgh, and confute personally many false aspersions made against me by him and others. Write me how the main [cock-fight] went; how you came on in it; if my black cock fought and gained, &c., &c.

As I can give you no directions how to write me, you'll please seal your letter, give it to Robert Smith, and he will deliver it to my sister, who will take care that it be conveyed safe to me wherever I may happen to be at the time, for I will give such directions that everything that is sent to me shall be forwarded from place to place until it come to my hand. I have lived now eighteen days on board of ship, and in good health and spirits, although very bad when I came on board, having my tongue and throat in one ulcer, not a bit of skin upon either, and the medicines I took in my friend's and by her direction (for she is one of experience), just beginning to operate; but I found it necessary, at all events, to remove, so I underwent a complete salivation on board ship. During all my trials since I left Edinburgh, my spirits nor my presence of mind never once forsook me, for which I have reason to be thankful. My best compliments to Mrs Henderson, and I will order payment of the two guineas as soon as I have accounts from the gentleman I have intrusted with my affairs; let her not be anxious about it, for, if I live, it shall be paid.

The letter breaks here into a second part:

Dear Michael

I am very uneasy on account of Mrs. Grant and my three children by her; they will miss me more than any other in Scotland. May God, in His infinite goodness, stir up some friendly aid for their support, for it is not in my power at present to give them the smallest assistance; yet I think they will not absolutely starve in a Christian land where their father once had friends, and who was always liberal to the distressed. I beg you will order the inclosed to be delivered into her own hand; and I will take it kind if Mrs. Henderson will send for her and give her good advice. I wish she may be enabled to keep what little furniture she has together.

I think she should endeavour to get her youngest daughter Jean sent to Aberdeen to her friends, where she will be well brought up, and I will order an yearly board to be paid for her, perhaps six pounds per annum; it will be an ease to Mrs Grant, and better for the child. My eldest daughter Cecill should be put apprentice to the milliner or mantua-making business; but I wish she could learn a little writing and arithmetic first. I wish to God some of my friends would take some charge of Cecill; she is a fine, sensible girl, considering the little opportunity she has had for improvement.

I have been now eighteen days on board, and I expect to land somewhere to-morrow. The ship rolls a good deal, and it is with some difficulty I get this wrote, and my paper being exhausted I shall conclude this epistle. Please make my compliments to Mr Clark, and a few other friends, and in particular, to Mr Balmano, and acquaint him I glimed the scrive [burned the letter] I had of him. He is a gentleman I have a great regard for. Pray do not forget writing me a long letter.

I am, Dear Michael,

For ever your's.

W. B.

Pray do not show this scroll to any but your wife.

A Significant Slip-up

After Brodie's arrest and arrival back in London, one of his two trunks was opened to reveal a bundle of papers that included two draft letters or (as they were then described) 'unsigned scrolls', which were also unaddressed but obviously intended for friends in Edinburgh. They contained comments that author William Roughead (*Trial of Deacon Brodie*) called 'compromising', adding, 'it is difficult to see why he had preserved such documents.' The most important slip-up can be seen in the letter below, when its writer says: 'Whatever these men may say, I had no hand in any of their depredations, excepting the last, which I shall ever repent …' It is a clear admission of involvement in the key crime that was being considered by the court and, as such, hugely incriminating. It was merely required to establish that it was in Brodie's handwriting, and this was duly done.

My dear Sir,

By short instructions sent me when I left London, which I think were drawn up in my cousin Milton's hand, I was forbid writing to any one in Britain, Mr Walker excepted, for a year or two; but this order, if necessary,

I find it not easy for me to comply with, for I must correspond with my friends in whatever part of the globe I am, and I hope they will do so with me, and write them when an opportunity offers. I have gone through much, in every sense of the word. – J. D. and M.

I wrote Mr Walker from this the 12th current. I received an answer the 18th, and wrote again the 23rd current, and upon receiving his next I hope to be enabled to embark in the first ship for America, to whatever port she is bound, which will probably be Charlestown, South Carolina, as there is a ship lying-to for that port; and notwithstanding the climate is very hot, and not so salutary to British constitutions, especially at the time I will arrive, which will be about the dog days. I will settle there if I think I can do better than at Philadelphia or New York. Longevity to me is now no object; but, at any rate, I will be at New York, and I hope to find there letters, and, if possible, some clothes and tools, otherwise I will be badly off indeed.

It grieves me to hear my creditors were so rigorous hasty, but well pleased on hearing the deed and conveyance had the proper effect. I hope all my creditors will be paid, and a reversion, which can be no object to the Crown. Were an application made to the Solicitor, and, if needful, a supplication in my name to his mother, and uncle the Treasurer, perhaps it might be a means either of quieting or getting easier through the threatened suit with the Crown; but this is only my idea.

At any rate, if my clothes and tools must go to sale, a proper assortment of tools, put into my best chest, might be put up in one lot, and my wearing apparel and linens in another lot. They are worth more to me than any one, and I think few in Edinburgh will bid for them if known they are designed for me; but if any one bids their value, in God's name let them have them, otherwise I hope they will be bought for me. I wish it were possible for me to know, before I left this, if I might expect them at New York; if otherwise, I will be under an absolute necessity of laying out what little money may remain, after paying my passage and clearing my board and lodging here, to my last shilling, and buying a few necessaries, otherwise I will land almost naked; and, if possible, to reach a few tools, both of which, I am informed, are £50 per cent, dearer in America than here.

I received from Mr Walker, in all, £12 16s., and he would pay something for three days I slept in Mr Rose's, though I am at present three guineas in debt to my landlord, and not a stiver in my pocket for four days past. This is the dearest place I was ever in.

I beg I may hear from you when at New York, and, if directed to Mr John Dixon, to the care of the Reverend Dr. Mason, I will certainly receive it (as I know no other name there to desire you to direct it to), for I will certainly call there, whatever part I land or settle in, in expectation of letters, &c., and, in particular, a long letter from you, in which please answer the following questions without reserve. I am prepared to hear the worst: – How does my dear sisters keep their health? I hope the shock of my departure, and what followed, has not injured either of them in health. How did they stand it? Where does my sister Jeany live? I hope there is no alteration in Mr Sheriff's friends to my dear Jamie. If money is an object, it is all in his favour. How is Mr and Mrs Grant, and Mr William, to whom I am for ever much obliged for settling my passage. It was a deep cut, but the more I am obliged to him and shall never forget it. He is a feeling and a generous gentleman.

I am sorry I cannot say so much of my cousin Milton, although he, too, was anxious for my off-going. How does my uncle and Mrs. Rintoull keep their health? From his conduct and repeated expressions, I never had much reason to expect anything from him, but now far less, although I be more needful. I believe few at my age ever went out more so. At present I am destitute of everything. I can put every article I have upon my back, and in my pocket. How does Mrs Campbell and her son's family?

Who were the most forward of my creditors to attach? How does my affairs turn out in the whole? If Robert Smith [his foreman] is employed, has he been active and attentive? He would need to be looked after, although he may be useful; and any news or alterations relating to my friends that may have happened.

What has been done, or likely to be done, with the two unfortunate men, Smith and Ainslie, and the greater villain, John Brown alias Humphry Moore? Was John Murray alias Jack Tasker [the Chesterfield fence] brought from England? Whatever these men may say, I had no hand in any of their depredations, excepting the last, which I shall ever repent, and the keeping such company, although I doubt not but all will be laid to me. But let me drop this dreadful subject. S. W., T. L., R. S., J. M., J. S.

An Ironic Comment

In the following draft letter, the second from his trunk, he said it again, in slightly different words: 'I had no direct concern in any of their depredations, excepting the last fatal one, by which I lost ten pounds in cash.' Unlike the general, damning admission, the word 'direct' had obviously been thought about – and scored out. And there seemed to be another general confession of bad behaviour in his statement that 'I often went in retregard'. His handwriting was also established in this case, and it seems ironic that – as a man who was to be historically notorious for his double life – here he caustically commented that his foreman 'is double and would need looking after'.

Pray write me what is become of Anne Grant, and how is her children disposed of. Cecill [their elder daughter] is a sensible, clever girl, considering the little opportunity she has had of improving. My dear little Willie [their son] will be, if I can judge, a brave and hardy boy.

Jean [their younger daughter] is her mother's picture, and too young to form any opinion of. What has become of Jean Watt? She is a devil and I can form no opinion of Frank or his young brother; but pray write me how they are disposed of.

If you please, write me what is become of the two unhappy men, Smith, and his wife, and Ainslie. Are they yet? Is their trial come on? and the greater villain John Brown alias Humphry Moore? I shall ever repent keeping such company, and whatever they may allege, I had no direct concern in any of their depredations, excepting the last fatal one, by which I lost ten pounds in cash; but I doubt not but all will be laid to my charge, and some that I never heard of.

The following is written at the foot of the page:

I often went in a retregard. I have been all my life in a reteregard motion.

And what follows is written on the other side:

Does Mr [William] Martin stand his bargain? Is any of my late property sold? Who is making out my accounts? Has Robert Smith been useful and active in my affairs? He is double and would need looking after.

Perhaps, in the course of making out and settling my accounts, some questions may occur that I may solve. If there is any such, please write them down, and I will answer them in course. Has any settlement taken place with Mr Little? I am afraid my affairs will be a laborious task to you; but I hope all my creditors will be paid, and a reversion.

If all my moveables are not yet sold, I beg my clothes and linen, and a set of useful tools may be preserved for me; they are worth more to me than another.

I wrote more fully some time ago to Mr Walker on this head, and also Mr Sheriff, the 8th April; but I know not if he received it. Pray let me know if he did, and how he stands affected towards me. Whatever be his sentiments, I shall always esteem him and regard him as my brother, but I shall never write another friend until I hear from you, and have your opinion how they will take it.

Pray, did Captain Dent ever make any discovery who I was when he arrived at Leith.

[Signed]: ??????????

To Auld Acquaintance

There were also, of course, the less contentious and less personal letters he managed to write from his prison cell to old acquaintances rather than friends or relatives, and one of them – written shortly before his trial but showing his sense of humour to be still intact – was addressed to his one-time fellow town councillor, 'Don. Smith Esq.' ...

Edinburgh, 17th August, 1788

Dear Sir,

The nails of my toes and fingers are not quite so long as Nebuchadnezzar's are said to have been, although long enough for a Mandarine, and much longer than I find convenient. I have tried several experiments to remove this evil without effect, which no doubt you'll think says little for your Ward's ingenuity; and I have the mortifications to perceive the evil daily increasing.

Dear Sir, as I intend seeing company abroad in a few days, I beg as soon as convenient you'll take this matter under consideration, and only, if necessary, consult my Guardian and Tutor sine qua non; and I doubt not but you'll devise some safe and easy method of operation that may give me a temporary relief. Perhaps the faculty may prescribe a more radical cure.

Dear sir, if not disagreeable to you, I'll be happy to see you. You'll be sure to find me at home, and all hours are equally convenient.

Believe me to be, with great esteem,

Your most affectionate Ward and very humble servant

WILL. BRODIE

As the hour of his 'dissolution' drew near – indeed, on the very morning of his execution – Deacon Brodie wrote to Edinburgh's Lord Provost [Mayor] asking that his body be delivered to his friends to be 'decently dressed and interred'. This was readily granted – unlike his earlier last-minute pleas for help to the Right Hon Henry Dundas (Viscount Melville) and the Duchess of Buccleuch. All three letters appear in the final chapter of this book.

The Will, with Five Days to Go

For most people, the writing of a last will and testament is surely a matter of serious reflection and balanced intent, 'being of sound mind and body'. Perhaps that time-honoured phrase is brought into sharp focus on a reading of the sardonic will of William Brodie written in the Tolbooth prison, a month after he was sentenced to death and five days before he stepped up to the gallows:

I, William Brodie, late Deacon of the Wrights in Edinburgh, and sometime member of the Town council of said burgh, considering the certainty of my death and the propriety and expediency of recommending my memory by some good offices to my friends when I am no more, do hereby execute my last will and testament in manner following, that is to say –

1. Having a Royal Successor to my means and estates, an nothing else to dispose of but my good and bad qualifications, I dispose of these as follows:–

To the Right Honourable, (for a few days to come), John Grieve, Esq., I give and bequeath all my political knowledge in securing magistrates and packing corporations, hoping he will use the same in effecting a seat for himself at a certain board, to which he has long had an eye, on the first vacancy.

2. To James Donaldson, I freely bequeath my sobriety and good breeding, which may save him from being kicked out of company on occasion of his petulance and ill-manners, as was lately the case at Archers' Hall.

3. My charity and good deeds I humbly bequeath to the ministers of the Gospel, in Scotland, with this injunction, that they do not retail them among their hearers, but put them in practice amongst themselves.

4. To the Magistrates of Edinburgh, present and to come, I leave and bequeath all my knowledge of the law, which may prevent their being under the necessity in future of borrowing from any of their Jameos [their clerks], who are as ignorant as themselves.

5. To my late landlord, William Charles Little of Liberton, Esq., I leave my whole stock of economy, pride, and self-conceit, knowing he has very little of his own.

6. To William Creech, bookseller, who has favoured the public with an account of my trial, I give and bequeath my honour and generosity, referring the world to the note prefixed to Mr Morrison's appendix.

7. To Hamilton, the chimney sweep, I leave and bequeath my dexterity in cards and dice, which may enable him to refund himself of the five guineas, two half-guineas, and six shillings which he prosecuted me for, when he meets a pigeon, which I advertise him he is not likely to do either at Clerk's or Michael Henderson's.

8. To my good friends and old companions, Brown and Ainslie, I freely bequeath all my bad qualities, not doubting, however, but their own will secure them a rope at last.

My neck now being about to embrace the halter, I would recommend it to all rogues, sharpers, thieves, and gamblers, whether in high or low station, to take care of theirs, by leaving-off their wicked practices, and becoming good members of Society in future.

Written with my own hand, and dated Sept. 26, 1788.

WILLM BRODIE

It had to be remarkable, did it not, that this unusual character could still employ his impish sense of humour when about to pay his debts to an aggrieved society? Why would his imminent confrontation with the Grim Reaper be anything for him or his relatives to laugh about? But there were, as we know, a good few dubious sides to William Brodie, and one of them was his innate inability to pay his debts on time.

6

THE TRIAL: YOU STAND ACCUSED

Theirs had been the worst of evil crimes. The calculated targeting and befriending of unsuspecting victims who would be persuaded to join in convivial drink marathons, then, when totally befuddled or asleep, end up being 'burked' – smothered and compressed about the chest until they realised (perhaps) that they were drawing their last, wide-eyed, silent-screaming breath. A series of sixteen such murders for money made the bodysnatcher-killers William Burke and William Hare the most notorious criminals in the annals of Edinburgh's history – thoroughly deserving of the death penalty, though the latter even managed to avoid it by turning Crown's evidence against his partner-in-crime.

But did William Brodie and George Smith deserve to be hanged after their trial exactly forty years before? However reprehensible their crimes, they were merely burglars and had not killed, nor even physically hurt, anyone. Certainly, a batch of loaded pistols had accompanied them on their most ambitious job – the robbing of Scotland's General Excise Office – and it could therefore be argued that there was a readiness, if not an intention, to shoot anyone getting in their way. But the weapons may have been there for romantic effect and, in the event, were not used. Indeed, the job itself was something of a damp discharge, yielding a lot less money than expected (see page 71) but was it, ultimately, the how-dare-they audaciousness of it that seeded the seriousness of the sentencing?

And despite the allegations of at least ten break-ins, the focus of their trial was constantly on that particular incident that had indelibly insinuated itself into the outraged minds of Edinburgh's citizenry, and particularly its legal establishment; all classes seemed utterly transfixed by the sharpness of the social and character contrasts displayed by Brodie: respectable town councillor by day, sleazy burglar by night. There was definitely a large school of resentment in all camps' thinking: not just theft but betrayal of class. Many thought: why shouldn't he pay the ultimate price for that?

It couldn't happen today, of course, no matter how shocked society might be by a crime short of murder; even back then – in the absence of a not-proven verdict or appeals procedures – there was the option of transportation to the Colonies, which was apparently never considered. But chief among the five judges on the bench was the Lord Justice Clerk, Lord Braxfield, a bulldog of a man with widely acknowledged common sense – being the grandson of an earl's gardener – but a fearsome reputation; indeed, he was often called 'The Hanging Judge'. And having been a friend of Brodie's father, he was not beyond passing his influence and opinion – that the son was guilty of disgracing the memory of the father – to his fellow judges: Lords Hailes, Eskgrove, Swinton and Stonefield.

And another move that would be seen as irregular today was Braxfield's choosing of the jury's fifteen male members, including William Creech, the bookseller and publisher who had been a resentful enemy of Brodie on the city council and who was to write and publish his own version of the trial only a few days after it ended.

Outside and in, the Court of Justiciary was overwhelmed by an excited public whose appetite for the trial had been whetted by the double-life tales and escape and capture of the main man, who was now being transported by sedan chair across Parliament Close from the Tolbooth prison; likewise, his co-accused. But neither of them could be seen, escorted as they were by 'sentinels of the City Guard on the right and left, with naked bayonets, and a sergeant's guard behind, with muskets and fixed bayonets' – responsible for keeping the parties apart. From the castle, a detachment of the 7th Regiment of Foot lined Parliament Square to ease the passage to court of lawyers and jurymen and help calm the great crowds.

What the public within the court eventually saw was a well-dressed, confident-looking Brodie emerge from the sedan chair to take his seat alongside a dejected-looking Smith. 'Mr Brodie was genteelly dressed in a new dark-blue coat, a fashionable fancy waistcoat, black satin breeches, and white silk stockings, a cocked hat, and had his hair fully dressed and powdered', according to a contemporary report, 'while Smith was poorly clothed, having had no money since his confinement, which had already lasted six months'.

The open-air crowds, meanwhile, took in the spectacle of the arrival of the scarlet-robed and full-wigged Braxfield, who had walked from his elegant home in George's Square to reach Parliament House in good time for the 9 a.m. start of the trial on the grey morning of Wednesday 27 August 1788. Inside the court, at the appointed hour and preceded by a macer bearing the Justiciary Mace, he led the five judges to their seats and nodded a greeting to the other main legal players in the drama: Ilay Campbell, the King's Advocate, leading for the prosecution, assisted by Solicitor General Dundas, a nephew of Henry Dundas (who had helped Braxfield to become Lord Justice Clerk) and advocates William Tait and James Wolfe Murray; for Smith's defence, advocates John Clerk and Robert Hamilton; and for Brodie's defence, the Dean of Faculty, Henry Erskine, along with advocates Alexander Wight and Charles Hay. There would be extra tension in court as these officers were divided by more than points of law: the defence team were all Whigs, while the prosecution and judges were Tories.

Was it the backing of Henry Erskine that had made Brodie so perky? The services of this 'chief ornament of the Scottish bar' had been, apparently secured by his friends and – as an enthusiast for fighting cocks – he is said to have commented, 'So now we've got the best cock that ever fought.' And according to the *Edinburgh Advertiser*, Brodie never lost his cool confidence: 'His behaviour during the whole trial was perfectly collected. He was respectful to the court, and when anything ludicrous occurred in the evidence he smiled as if he had been an indifferent spectator.'

The trial began with a reading of the charges against the two men:

WILLIAM BRODIE, sometime Wright and Cabinetmaker in Edinburgh, and GEORGE SMITH, sometime Grocer there, both prisoners in the Tolbooth of Edinburgh, You are indicted and accused at the instance of Ilay Campbell, Esq., His Majesty's Advocate, for His Majesty's interest: THAT ALBEIT, by the laws of this, and of every well-governed realm, THEFT, more especially when attended with house-breaking, and when committed by breaking into a house used or kept as an Excise Office, or other public office, under cloud of night, and from thence abstracting and stealing money, is a crime of an heinous nature, and severely punishable: YET TRUE IT IS, AND OF VERITY, That You, the said William Brodie, and George Smith, are both, and each, or one or other of You, guilty actors, or art and part, of the said crime, aggravated as aforesaid: IN SO FAR AS, upon the night of the 5th day of March, last, in this present year of our Lord 1788, or upon one or other of the days or nights of that month, or of February immediately preceding, or of April immediately following. You, the said William Brodie, and George Smith, did, by means of false keys, or other instruments, wickedly and feloniously break into the house in which the General Excise Office for Scotland was then kept, in Chessels's buildings, on the south side of the High-street of Canongate of Edinburgh, within the royalty or liberties of the city of Edinburgh, and county of Edinburgh,

'Doomed to death' … William Brodie (right) and his co-accused, George Smith.

How it looked back then: the head of Brodie's Close in the Lawnmarket, sketched by Bruce J. Home.

The foot of the close, by the same artist.

The Old Excise Office, Chessel's Court, Canongate, in a sketch by Bruce J. Home. This was the site of Brodie's failed armed raid of 1788 that led to his downfall.

A cock-fighting match in Edinburgh, attended by Deacon Brodie.

Thus we poor Cocks, exert our skill & Brav'ry
For idle Gulls, and Kites, that trade in Knav'ry

A COCK FIGHTING MATCH
Between the Counties of Lanark and Haddington.

The Brodie-crafted cabinet that stood in the young Robert Louis Stevenson's bedroom and inspired him to created Jekyll and Hyde.

Brodie's lantern and some of 'his' keys are now kept in the Bank of Scotland's Museum on the Mound.

Brodie was arrested in Amsterdam under the name John Dixon and held in what is now the Dam Square royal palace … where, intriguingly, four cast-iron lamp posts bear the name Dixon. (Picture: Norman MacDonald)

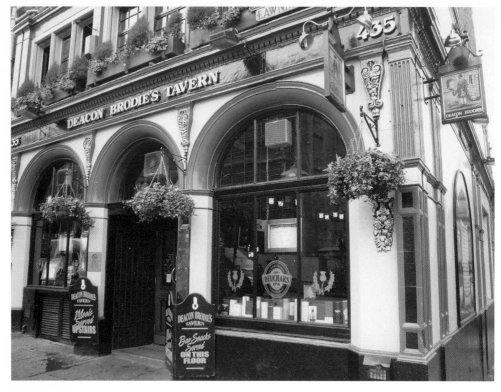

The popular Deacon Brodie's Tavern on Edinburgh's Royal Mile …

… where the exterior name boards depict the contrasting two sides of the original's character.

Deacon's House Cafe now occupies the site of Brodie's one-time home and workshop.

Hanged: George Smith.

'Bulldog' hanging judge, Lord Braxfield.

Not quite gone. The human-sized effigy of Deacon Brodie that stands outside Brodie's Close today.

and did thence feloniously abstract and steal money, to the amount of Sixteen pounds Sterling, or thereby, consisting partly of banknotes, and partly of silver and halfpence. And You, the said George Smith, having been afterwards apprehended, and brought before Archibald Cockburn, Esq., Sheriff-depute of the county of Edinburgh, did, in his presence, emit three several declarations; the first of date the 8th day of March, the second of date the 10th day of March, and the third of date the 19th day of March, all in this present year of our Lord 1788: And having afterwards been brought before John Stewart, Esq., Sheriff-substitute of the said county, You did, in his presence, emit a fourth declaration, of date the 17th day of July, likewise in this present year 1788: The first of which declarations was signed by the said Archibald Cockburn, the second and third by you, the said George Smith, and the said Archibald Cockburn, and the fourth by you, the said George Smith, and the said John Stewart.

AND FURTHER, You, the said William Brodie, having, in the month of March last, when the said George Smith was committed to prison, left Edinburgh, and fled from this country; and having afterwards been brought back, and taken into custody, did, upon the 17th day of July, in this present year 1788, in presence of the said Archibald Cockburn, Esq., emit a declaration, which was signed by you, the said William Brodie, and the said Archibald Cockburn; the whole of which declarations, together with a letter written by You, the said William Brodie, and signed John Dixon, dated at Flushing, Tuesday, 8th April, 1788, twelve o'clock forenoon, and addressed to Mr Matthew Sheriff, upholsterer, Edinburgh; another letter, or two letters, on one sheet of paper, written by You the said William Brodie, and signed with your initials, dated Thursday, 10th April, 1788, and addressed to Mr Michael Henderson, Grassmarket, stabler, Edinburgh; an unsigned scroll, or copy of a letter, in the hand-writing of You, the said William Brodie, marked No. 1 without date or address; another unsigned scroll, or copy of a letter, in the hand-writing of You, the said William Brodie, marked

No. 2 without date or address; an account, or state, in the hand-writing of You, the said William Brodie, entitled, "A state of my affairs, as near as I can make out at present from memory, having no other assistance"; a letter, dated London, 1st May, 1788, signed Lee, Strachan, and Co. and addressed to Mess. Eml. Walker and Co., merchants, Philadelphia; a gold watch, with a chain, seal, and key; a chest, or trunk, containing various articles; a five-pound bank-note; an iron coulter of a plough; two iron wedges; an iron crow; a pair of curling irons or toupee tongs; a spur; a dark lanthorn; a pair of pistols; several false keys and picklocks; and two spring-saws; are all to be used in evidence against You the said William Brodie and George Smith; and, for that purpose, will be lodged in the hands of the clerk of the High Court of Justiciary, before which You are to be tried, in order that You may have an opportunity of seeing the same: AT LEAST, time and place foresaid, the said house in which the General Excise Office for Scotland was then kept as aforesaid, was feloniously broke and entered into, and a sum of money feloni-ously and theftuously taken and stolen therefrom as aforesaid; and You the said William Brodie, and George Smith, above complained upon, are both, and each, or one or other of You, guilty thereof, actor or actors, or art and part. ALL WHICH, or part thereof, being found proven by the verdict of an assize, before the Lord Justice-General, Lord Justice-Clerk, and Lords Commissioners of Justiciary, You, the said William Brodie, and George Smith, OUGHT to be punished with the pains of law, to deter others from committing the like crimes in all time coming.

ILAY CAMPBELL

(His Majesty's Advocate, for His Majesty's interest)

The prisoners were signalled to stand while Lord Braxfield asked: 'William Brodie, you have heard the indictment raised against you by His Majesty's Advocate – are you guilty of the crime therein charged, or not guilty?'

Brodie replied: 'My Lord, I am not guilty.'

'George Smith – are you guilty of the crime therein charged, or not guilty?'

Smith replied: 'Not guilty, my Lord.'

The judge then swore in the fifteen jury members five at a time, repeating: 'You swear by Almighty God, and as you shall answer to God at the great day of judgment, that you will truth say, and no truth conceal, so far as you are to pass upon this assize.'

The fifteen were: Robert Forrester, banker; Robert Allan, banker; Henry Jamieson, banker; John Hay, banker; William Creech, bookseller; James Carfrae, merchant; John Kinnear, banker; William Fettes, merchant; John Milne, founder; Dunbar Pringle, tanner; Thomas Campbell, merchant; Francis Sharp, merchant; James Donaldson, printer; John Hutton, stationer; and Thomas Cleghom, coachmaker.

There were just short of 100 witnesses for the prosecution, while those standing up in Brodie's defence numbered a mere twenty-five. Packed as it was with characters, curiosity, opinions, facts, sharp legal combat and an intense interest that still captivates the people of Edinburgh and beyond, the trial lasted a mere twenty-one hours after entering early Thursday morning then taking a few hours' break before seeing the jury's verdict delivered at 1 p.m.

'Intense interest' will always be a subjective term for whoever uses it, of course, and in selecting and commenting on several aspects of the trial – without recording the entire trial verbatim – this writer hopes readers will feel its essential flavour has been imparted.

Excise Office Witnesses

Did anyone see the Brodie gang robbing the Excise Office? Not quite. While the project faltered because of the unexpected return to the office of Excise Deputy Solicitor James Bonnar, a hunched figure in a long, dark coat was not recognised. But the incident prompted Brodie to make a sharp exit with slim pickings. The other gang members, John Brown, George Smith and Andrew Ainslie, also got away, and as news of the burglary at Chessels Court spread around the city, it seemed unlikely that any of them would be caught – until Brown decided to confess to Sheriff Clerk William Middleton almost a week later. He offered information on all the gang's crimes in return for the advertised reward and a King's Pardon, which, under English law, would wipe clean all his past criminal records. At first he named only Ainslie and Smith as his accomplices. But it was on hearing this, and perhaps expecting his name to arise at any moment, that Brodie made his great, if short-lived, escape from justice.

Questioned at the trial, the following people could not put names to the shadowy figures who broke so crassly into their usually well-ordered head-down routine lives on the night of 5 March 1788:

James Bonnar, deputy-solicitor of Excise: I recollect having occasion to call at the Excise Office at about half-past eight in the evening, and as I thought it was probable that there might be still some person in the office, I went straight forward to the door without calling for the key, and finding the door on the latch, I opened it and went in. Just as I entered, a man, who appeared to be dressed in a black coat and cocked hat, stepped out. He seemed to be in a hurry, and I stepped aside to give way to him. He was a square-built man, and was rather taller than me. I took no suspicion, thinking it was some of the people belonging to the office, detained later than usual. I went upstairs to the solicitor's office, and into the room in which I usually write. I remained there about ten minutes, came down again, and then went away. I saw no person either in the entry or the court as I came out.

William Mackay, guard at the Excise Office: I went to the office at the usual hour, which was a little before ten o'clock at night. I found one of the leaves of the outer door open, and the passage door and the door of the cashier's room also open; and upon making this discovery I went to Mr Dundas, the housekeeper's, and inquired of the maid who had been last at the office, as the doors were open. The maid answered John Duncan, the last witness, had left it about a quarter after eight o'clock. Mr Dundas's son, hearing me make this inquiry, asked what was the matter. When I told him that the door was broke open, he said, 'Then, something worse is done.' Immediately Mr and Mrs Dundas and the whole family went into the office with me and examined the cashier's room; we found all the desks and presses broke open, and the coulter of a plough, and two iron wedges, lying in the room; and we likewise found a spur in the hall, with part of the leather of it torn. Mr Dundas immediately sent me for Mr Alexander Thomson, the accountant. I found Mr Thomson, and he returned with me to the Office.

Alexander Thomson, accountant of Excise: I remember that the Excise Office was broke into on Wednesday, the 5th of March last. When I left the office at the usual hour that night, about eight o'clock, I locked the door of the cashier's room before I left, and carried the key away with me. I saw John Duncan, the doorkeeper, in the hall as I came out. I left in two concealed drawers below the desk about £600 sterling, and in the desk itself £15 16s. 3d., being two-thirds of the proceeds of a seizure sent from Greenock, to be divided amongst three people. About ten o'clock the same evening the office porter, or watchman, came to me and informed me that the Excise Office had been broken into.

I immediately repaired to the office, and found Mr Dundas, the housekeeper, and Mr Pearson, the secretary, there; and, along with them, I examined the premises. The outer door and the passage door appeared to have been opened without violence, but the door of the cashier's room seemed to have been forced with a lever or other instrument; the door of a small press in the room appeared likewise to have been forced open, and a few shillings, and some stamps for receipts that were in it, carried off. The key of my desk, which I usually kept in this place, had likewise been taken out, and the desk opened with it. The £15 odds, which I had left in the desk, were gone, and also a receipt for £7 18s. 2d., but the concealed drawers, in which the £600 was contained, were untouched. These drawers cannot be opened without first opening the desk, and the keyhole is concealed by a slip of wood, which might escape a slight observer. Accordingly it had remained untouched, although the key of it lay in the desk. Behind the door there was left the coulter of a plough and two iron wedges.

Laurence Dundas, housekeeper of the Excise Office: There was a practice, previous to the time when, the Excise Office was broke into, of locking the door betwixt eight and nine o'clock at night, and lodging the key in my house, and of putting a watch upon it at ten o'clock. I remember that upon Wednesday, the 5th of March last, the door was locked at the usual hour, and the key left by John Duncan at my house. A little before ten o'clock that night, William Mackay, the porter employed to watch the office, came to my house and gave information that the office had been broke open. I immediately went to the office, and found the outer door, the passage door, and the door of the cashier's room, all open. This last-mentioned door seemed to have been forced with some instrument. Within the room I found the coulter of a plough and two iron wedges … Every drawer in the room, except the money drawers, seemed to have been forced open. I immediately sent for Mr Thomson, the accountant, and Mr Pearson, the secretary, and both immediately came to the office. Mr Thomson told me he had about £17 in his desk, which he supposed was all gone, but he hoped that the money drawers were safe. The key of the money drawers was found amongst others lying in the desk.

Janet Baxter, servant to Adam Pearson, assistant secretary of the Excise: I was out upon a message about eight o'clock that night and, returning homewards, I met an acquaintance, with whom I conversed for a little in the entry to Chessels Buildings, in which my master lived. I then went down the close, and on my way down I saw a man, dressed in a whitish great-coat and slouch hat, leaning over the rails at the entry to the court, and, judging him to be a light or suspicious person, I was afraid of him, and ran into my master's house.

So far, the evidence led against Brodie and Smith was mostly circumstantial. As the Excise officer Bonnar had not been able to identify the fleeing figure as Brodie – although he knew him – no observation had actually placed the city councillor at the scene. All three of Brodie's gang had now confessed – and although his co-accused Smith had withdrawn his confession, the gang leader's fate could very well depend now on the admissibility of evidence from Brown and Ainslie.

Admissible ... or Not?

The admissibility of certain persons' evidence was to test the court's legal brains and patience to the limit, especially in view of bargains made with Brown and Ainslie, who, having initially held his tongue in reluctance to incriminate Brodie, had been given the choice of testifying against him or hanging. 'No man could withstand such a temptation,' said the Dean of Faculty Henry Erskine, 'and it is impossible that the court can receive the testimony of a witness in such circumstances.'

But unsurprisingly, despite such strong defence objections to the deal – finally overruled by Braxfield – Ainslie became a Crown witness and was called to speak.

One not allowed to speak was Brown's wife Mary, not so much because of her relationship with him but because of a misspelling of her name on the witness sheet.

Brown himself, however, also got the green light despite the defence position that corroborative evidence from him should not be allowed because he was 'infamous' under Scots law, being a known criminal and so not permitted to bear witness. However, the prosecution had obtained a King's Pardon, which, under English law, absolved him of all previous wrongdoings.

These decisions were quietly enraging John Clerk, the young defence counsel (for Smith), who had clearly resolved to keep his powder dry before creating an almighty explosion towards the end of proceedings.

In the meantime, however, the other two 'absolved' members of Brodie's gang stood to give evidence that could only be seen to involve and damn their erstwhile boss. Such as:

Andrew Ainslie: I am acquainted with both William Brodie and George Smith, the prisoners at the bar, and also with John Brown alias Humphry Moore. I remember that the Excise Office was broke into upon Wednesday, the 5th of March last. I knew before that that it was to be broken into, but how long I cannot tell. Brown and the prisoners and I frequently talked of it before, and Brown and I went often to the Excise Office in the evenings in order to observe at what hour the people left it, and in consequence of repeated observations we discovered that the door was usually locked about eight o'clock and that there were two men, an old and a younger man, who came night about to watch the office about ten o'clock. Afterwards Brown and I went out one afternoon to a house at Duddingston, where we drank a bottle of porter, and saw a woman whom I took to be the landlady. We then went to a field in the neighbourhood, from which we took the coulter of a plough and two iron wedges, which we carried to the Salisbury Crags and hid there. At this time there was a black dog in company with us. We had fixed on Wednesday, the 5th of March, for committing the said robbery, and allowed the coulter to remain in Salisbury Crags until about six o'clock of the evening of that day, when Brown and I, it being then dusk, went out and brought the coulter of the plough to the house of the prisoner, George Smith, on purpose to use it in breaking into the Excise Office.

We found Smith at home, and we expected Mr Brodie to join us and to accompany us to the Excise Office. Brodie did not come until a good while after, when he joined us in the room above-stairs in Smith's house. Mr Brodie was at this time dressed in a light-coloured great-coat, with black clothes below (in which I had often seen him before), and a cocked hat. When he came in he had a pistol in his hand, and was singing a verse of what I understood to be a flash song. By a flash song I mean a highwayman's song. We spoke together concerning the Excise Office; and it was settled upon that I should go before to the Excise Office and get within the rails and observe when the people went out. I went there accordingly a little before eight o'clock, carrying the coulter of the plough with me, and waited till I saw the porter come out with a light and lock the outer door. In a short while thereafter Smith came to me and asked if the people were all gone, and when 1 informed him that they were gone out Smith then went forward and opened the door with a key, which, I had heard him say, he had previously made for it, and went into the office. In about five minutes thereafter Brodie came down the close, and when I told him that Smith had gone in, but that Brown was not yet come, he went up the close again towards the street, and returned in a little with Brown, who said he had been dogging the old man who watched the office in order to see where he went, and that he had gone home.

Brown then asked me whether or not I had 'Great Samuel' – by which he meant the coulter. I told him I had, and gave it him through the rails, and he and Brodie then went down towards the door of the office and went in, as I supposed.

I had no arms myself, excepting a stick, but Smith had three loaded pistols. Brown two, and Brodie one; at least, I saw Brodie, when he came into Smith's house, have one in his hand. It had been previously settled amongst us, before leaving Smith's house, that Brodie was to stand in the inside of the outer door, and that Brown and Smith were to go into the office. I was to remain without to watch, and in case of danger, to give an alarm to Brodie, which

Brodie was to communicate to Brown and Smith. The signal of alarm agreed upon was to be given by me in this manner – a single whistle if one man appeared, so that they might be prepared to secure him; but if more than one man, or any appearance of danger, I was to give three whistles, in order that those within might make their escape by the door or by the back windows, as they thought best. I had an ivory whistle prepared for the purpose, which was given me by Mr Brodie in Smith's house in the afternoon.

I took my station within the rail and leaned down, so that no person either going in or coming out could see me. Some short while after Brodie and Brown went into the office, a man came running down the close and went in also. I gave no alarm, for before I had time to think what I should do another man came immediately running out at the door and went up the court. In a very little afterwards, to my great surprise, a second man came out from the office. I got up and looked at him through the rails, and perceived that he was none of my three companions. I had not seen the other man who came out first so distinctly, owing to my lying down by the side of the parapet wall on which the rail is placed, in order that I might not be observed. I was afraid that we were discovered; and, as soon as the second man had gone up the close, I gave the alarm by three whistles as the agreed-on signal of retreat and ran up the close myself. I went down St John's Street and came round opposite to the back of the Excise Office, thinking to meet my companions coming out by the back way, having escaped from the windows. I remained there for some little time, and, not meeting with them, I then went directly to Smith's house. Finding none of them there, and Mrs Smith telling me that they were not yet come in, I went back to the Excise Office by the street, went down the close, saw the door open, and, finding everything quiet, I returned to Smith's, where I saw him and Brown. They accused me of not having given the alarm as I promised, and said that when they came out they found that Brodie had gone from his place. I told them what I had observed, and that I had given the alarm. I remained in Smith's only a few minutes and I did not see Brodie again that night.

John Brown: I have met Brodie often at Smith's house and other places. I know that the General Excise Office in Chessels's Buildings was broken into upon Wednesday, the 5th of March last; I was myself one of them that broke into it, and Andrew Ainslie and the two prisoners were along with me. George Smith and I were within the office, Brodie was at the door, and Andrew Ainslie was without, keeping watch. We had resolved three months before to break into it; and on the 30th of November last, the night on which the Free Masons made a public procession last winter. Smith, Ainslie, and I went to the Excise Office and unlocked the outer door with a false key. We went in together, and opened the inner door to the hall with a pair of toupee irons, but none of the keys we had would open the cashier's door. Smith said a coulter would be a good thing to open it with. Thinking it too late to remain longer, we came out again; but we could not lock the outer door with the key, and therefore left it unlocked. Last spring Ainslie and I went to Duddingston, and drank a bottle of porter in a house there; afterwards we went into a field in the neighbourhood, in which there were two ploughs, and carried off the coulter of one of them, which we hid in Salisbury Crags.

On the evening of the 5th of March last, which was two or three days afterwards, when it was about dusk, Ainslie and I went out to Salisbury Crags for the coulter, and brought it in with us to Smith's house. Smith was at home, but Brodie was not yet come, although we expected him. The hour at which we had agreed to meet was seven, but he did not come until near eight. The purpose of our meeting was to go and rob the Excise Office that night. We were in Smith's room above-stairs when Brodie joined us, and we there drank some gin and Black Cork, and ate some herrings and chicken. By Black Cork I mean Bell's beer. Mr Brodie was then dressed in black; in the preceding part of the day I saw him in white or light-coloured clothes. I do not remember that he had a great-coat on when he came to us at Smith's in the evening. When he entered the room he took a pistol from his pocket, and repeated the verse of a song of Macheath's from a play, words like – 'We'll turn our lead into gold' or such like.

After we were all met together, it was agreed upon that Ainslie should remain on the outside of the Excise Office, within the rails, with a whistle, to give the alarm in case of danger; that Brodie was to be stationed within the outer door for the same purpose; and that Smith and I should go into the cashier's room. Accordingly, Ainslie left Smith's first, and in some time after I followed. Brodie was not disguised but Smith and I had crapes in our pocket, and Smith had likewise a wig, which, I believe, had once belonged to Brodie's father. When I came to the mouth of the entry to Chessels's Buildings, I met the old man who usually locked the door coming out, and went after him and saw him go home. My reason for so doing was to see that he had not gone on an errand and to return. When I came back to the court I met Brodie in the entry, who told me that Smith had gone into the office, and desired me to go in. I went down the close with him, saw Ainslie at his post, and received the coulter, or 'Great Samuel', from him, and carried it in with me to the office. I found the outer door open and Smith in the hall. The outer door of the cashier's room was opened by Smith with a pair of curling irons, and I assisted him to force open the inner door of the cashier's room with the coulter and a small iron crow.

After we got in, Smith, who had a dark lanthorn with him, opened every press and desk in the room where he suspected there was any money; some by violence and others with keys which we found in the room. We continued there about half-an-hour, and found about sixteen pounds of money in a desk in the cashier's room, which we carried away with us. It consisted of two five-pound notes, six guinea notes, and some silver. We heard some person come upstairs, and cocked our pistols, which were loaded with powder and ball. Smith said he supposed it was some of the clerks going into one of the rooms. We heard no whistle while we were in the office. When we came downstairs, Brodie and Ainslie were both gone. We left the outer door of the Excise Office unlocked, and carried the key away with us. We then came up to the Canongate, and went across it, and down another street a little below – Young's Street. I stopped in the middle of the last street, pulled off my great-coat and gave it to Smith. I then returned, went down to the Excise Office door, where everything seemed to be quiet; afterwards I went to Smith's house, where in a little I was joined by Smith, and soon afterwards by Ainslie. I did not remain there long, when Smith recommended it to me and Ainslie to go over to Fraser's house in the New Town, that we might avoid suspicion; and we went accordingly. I knew at the time that Smith was making a key for the outer door of the Excise Office. [*Here the witness was shown a key.*]

That is the key he so made, and with which he opened the door. We had three pair of pistols along with us, all of which were previously loaded by Smith with powder and ball.

[*Here the said pistols were shown to the witness.*] These are a pair of them, but whether that pair was carried to the Excise Office by Smith or me I cannot say. I saw Mr Brodie have a pistol in his hand in Smith's house. When Brodie came to Smith's first that night he brought with him some small keys, and a double pick-lock, which we all looked at. [*Here the pick-lock libelled on was shown.*]

This is the same that was used on that occasion. On Friday, the 7th of March, I was sent for to Smith's house. Brodie, Smith, and Ainslie were there, and the money which we got in the Excise Office was then equally divided between us. I got about four pounds from Brodie to my share. I saw all the money in Smith's room above-stairs before it was divided, and there were two five-pound bank-notes amongst it. On the same Friday evening, I went with Smith and Ainslie to Drysdale's, in the New Town, and saw Smith change one of the five-pound notes there, when purchasing a ticket for his wife in the mail-coach to Newcastle. I went to William Middleton on Friday night, the 7th of March last, and told him that I wished to make a discovery as to the late robberies; he carried me the same night to Mr Scott, the Procurator-Fiscal, but I did not at that time mention anything of Brodie's concern in them. The next day I was sent to England to trace some goods taken from Inglis & Horner's shop. I returned on the 15th of March, and was the same day examined by the Sheriff. I was informed that Smith had emitted a declaration, informing of Brodie's guilt, in consequence of which he (Brodie) had absconded, and then for the first time I mentioned that Mr Brodie had been concerned with us.

Ainslie informed Smith and me that he had seen two men come up the close before he quitted his post at the Excise Office and went away. Smith carried the money that was found in the Excise Office away with him, and he afterwards gave it to Brodie, who made a fair division of it on the Friday. On the Thursday I did not see him.

Now, after so many name-checks, it wasn't, on the face of it, looking good for Brodie. But he still appeared relatively optimistic, hoping no doubt that the jury would see the gang 'witnesses' as just two rascals motivated to save themselves by defaming him. And in any case, he had always intended to mount a defence of alibi, so was keen to see those set to provide his required cover welcomed to the stand.

Alibis for Defence

Brodie's first alibi-provider was his brother-in-law, the upholsterer Matthew Sheriff, and for that reason – their close relationship – little notice was taken of his story. Indeed, in his later address to the jury the Lord Advocate Ilay Campbell could not hide his suspicions:

> This gentleman depones that he dined with Mr Brodie on Wednesday, the 5th of March, and that he was in company with him until eight o'clock that night …
>
> There was another gentleman, he tells you, who dined in company with the accused that day; and what appears to me to be a very odd circumstance, this gentleman is not called as a witness; nay, more, although Mr Sheriff recollects a great variety of other circumstances, he does not remember this gentleman's name. Why

is this gentleman not brought forward on this occasion? Why are not some of the servants of the house, or any other person, called to support Mr Sheriff's testimony? Mr Sheriff, then, is only a single witness, and from his near connection with the accused, he gives his evidence under circumstances that are suspicious, and therefore no weight can be allowed to it.

Would Brodie's mistress, her one-time servant and a neighbour at Libberton's Wynd be of more value to him? Jean Watt took the stand:

Jean Watt: I am well acquainted with the prisoner, William Brodie. I remember that on Wednesday, the 5th of March last, he came to my house just at the time the eight o'clock bell was ringing, and he remained in it all night, and was not out from the time he came in until a little before nine o'clock next morning. We went early to bed, about ten o'clock, as Mr Brodie complained that night of being much indisposed with a sore throat.

On the following Monday I heard that Mr Brodie was suspected of being concerned in the breaking into the Excise Office; that his house had been searched for him; and that he had gone away on the Sunday. This made me particularly recollect, and also because it was the last night Mr Brodie slept in my house. He slept with me that night. I have a family of children to him. I saw him again on the Saturday night afterwards, but not till then; and he was in my house in the forenoon of the Tuesday preceding.

Peggy Giles: I was servant to Mrs Watt, the preceding witness, last winter, and I remember that the prisoner, Mr Brodie, came to my mistress's house about eight o'clock at night of Wednesday, the 5th of March last, and that he slept there all night, and remained until about nine o'clock next morning. My mistress and Mr Brodie supped together early, about half-an-hour after eight o'clock, on bread and beer and a piece of cheese, for which I was sent out soon after Mr Brodie came in. I was out about ten minutes, and when I returned Mr Brodie was still in the house. I remember when he came in to have heard the eight o'clock bell ringing …

He was in bed when I arose in the morning, and I gave him water to wash his hands before he went out.

Helen Alison, wife of mason William Wallace: I reside in Libberton's Wynd, and I know the prisoner, Mr Brodie. I heard of his leaving Edinburgh in March last, and I remember to have seen him come down Jean Watt's stair a little before nine o'clock on the morning of the Thursday before he went off – the 6th of March. I was then standing at my own door at the foot of the stair; and I had Francis Brodie, the prisoner's son, a boy of about seven years of age, by the hand. As his father, Mr Brodie, passed he put a half-penny into the child's hand, and clapped him on the head. I said to the boy, 'Poor thing, thou hast been too soon out, or you would have seen your daddy at home'; he said, 'No, I have not been too soon out, for my daddy has been in the house all night.' After my husband got his breakfast, I went upstairs to Mrs Watt, and I said to her in a joking way, 'You will be in good humour today, as the good man has been with you all night.' She answered, 'He has; but, poor man, he has not been well of a sore throat.'

On the Monday following, I heard that there were messengers upstairs in Mrs Watt's, searching her house for Mr Brodie; and when I went up and was told what was the matter, I said to a sheriff-officer, then present, 'Dear sirs, who would have thought this would have happened, when I saw Mr Brodie come downstairs and give a bawbee to his own son on Thursday last?' To which the man answered, 'Indeed, few would have thought it.'

The Lord Advocate seemed equally unimpressed with these testimonies and later told the jury:

Jean Watt said she did not see Brodie from the Thursday morning, at nine o'clock, till the Saturday afternoon following, yet her maid said that he was twice in the house on the Thursday, in the forenoon and afternoon; though Sheriff said that Brodie was in his house on the Thursday from three o'clock in the afternoon till eleven o'clock at night. They can give no reason for fixing the night of his visit at Watt's house to be Wednesday night, except the subsequent flight of the prisoner; and therefore it may have been any other night in that week as well as the one condescended upon.

But, gentlemen, I have no occasion to dispute, and indeed, from the evidence of Helen Alison, I am inclined to believe that the prisoner went on the Wednesday night to Mrs Watt's house, and slept there that night; but I have heard nothing, allowing all the witnesses to have spoken what they believed to be true, to prove that he went there until after the crime was committed. Gentlemen, the circumstance which fixes the hour in the memory of both Mrs Watt and her servant is the ringing of a bell, and we all know that there is a bell that rings at ten o'clock as well as at eight. And it is very far from being improbable that they might both mistake the one bell for the other, either at the time, or afterwards, upon endeavouring to recollect the hour at which Brodie came to them. Allowing, therefore, that all the witnesses adduced by the prisoner are to be believed, there appears to be nothing in their testimony contradictory to the evidence of the prisoner's accession to the crime charged ...

Where to now? There was the matter of the letters sent from Holland. Would they help or hinder Brodie's chance of survival?

The Letters

While he was on the run and preparing to ship himself off to New York, William Brodie – clearly beginning to feel isolated and in need of some normal discourse – wrote several letters to friends and relatives. Three of them, mainly on domestic and professional concerns (page 110), were given for delivery to fellow-Scot

John Geddes (see previous chapter), with whom he shared the frustrating voyage from London to the Netherlands, while others were found in his trunk after his arrest. He had adopted the name John Dixon and none was properly signed as Brodie, so technically could not be attributed to him, but his handwriting on the scrolls that were shown in court was recognised by several witnesses to whom the style was familiar.

Was that enough to incriminate him? Not if the letters' content appeared to be entirely innocent, but one or two mistakes had been made, and one of them was to prove literally fatal. To recap, a Dixon-signed letter from Flushing to his brother-in-law Matthew Sheriff had this message scrawled on the back: 'Let my name and destination be a profound secret for fear of bad consequences' … which did not look so innocent. But the comment in another note (to 'my dear Sir') that truly sealed his fate was in reference to his fellow gang members: 'Whatever these men may say, I had no [*'direct'* – *excised*] hand in any of their depredations, excepting the last, which I shall ever repent …'

'Excepting the last'! This tacit admission of guilt would have any legal eagle swooping down on it as if on a trembling creature of prey. It looked as if Brodie had hung himself with his own words, and the prosecution merely had to tighten the rope.

But to return to the North Sea drama for a moment, let's look at the court-told stories of the initial letter-holders, the London solicitor Longlands and Brodie's reluctant shipmate, John Geddes:

Thomas Longlands: In June or July last I was employed by the officers of the Crown for Scotland to take such steps as appeared to me proper for the discovery of Mr Brodie. In consequence of this employment I called frequently at the Secretary of State's Office, and had several conversations with Mr Fraser, Under-Secretary in the office of Lord Carmarthen, and gave them the information I had received from Scotland.

I likewise waited upon Sir Sampson Wright, of the Public Office, Bow Street, whose assistance I judged necessary to call in as to the proper measures to be pursued. As the information received gave reason to suspect that Mr Brodie was at Flushing, Ostend, or some place in Holland, it was agreed upon to send a messenger immediately in search of him. Sir Sampson Wright recommended to me a Mr Groves from his office as a proper person to send to the Continent in search of Mr Brodie, and I accordingly despatched him with proper instructions.

Mr Groves traced Mr Brodie to Ostend, and learned that he had been there upon the 4th of June, His Majesty's birthday, and he was afterwards traced to Amsterdam, where he was apprehended, identified, and committed to prison. Upon proper application, he was delivered up to Mr Groves, and was brought from thence to London by him. Immediately upon his arrival at London he was examined before Sir Sampson Wright, and committed to Tothilfields Bridewell; some time afterwards he was sent to this country. I was present at the examination of the person brought back from Amsterdam, and I know the prisoner at the bar to be him. There was a trunk containing linens and a variety of other articles, belonging to Mr Brodie, brought with him from Amsterdam; and I received from Mr Cartmeal, one of the persons who came along with him, two watches, twenty crowns, and some other articles, which he said were found upon Mr Brodie; and the watch now upon the table I know to be one of them, having taken particular notice of the maker's name and number …

There was likewise another trunk belonging to Mr Brodie, which was sent over from Ostend by Sir John Potter, in consequence of a letter written to him in my presence by Mr Groves, after Brodie's return to London. This trunk, upon its being brought to London, was opened by Sir Sampson Thomas Wright in my presence, and in the course of examining the contents of it I discovered a wrapper with some papers, which I opened, and some of the papers appearing to me to be important, I transmitted them to Lord Advocate. [*Shown the unsigned scrolls*]. Both Sir Sampson Wright and I put our initials to them, and I am sure that these are the same …

John Geddes, tobacconist in Mid-Calder: I was in London in the month of March last, and my wife and I took our passage in the 'Endeavour', of Carron, Captain Dent, bound for Leith. We went on board on a Saturday, and the next day, Sunday, the vessel fell two or three miles down the river, and then we cast anchor at Blackwall. In the evening the master went ashore to get hands to man her, leaving me and my wife on board.

About twelve at night a passenger, who appeared sickly, came on board, in company with Mr Hamilton and Mr Pinkerton, two of the owners of the vessel, and another gentleman I did not know. These gentlemen remained about half an hour, and then all went ashore, except the passenger, who remained on board. He was dressed in a blue great-coat, with a red collar, round wig, black vest, breeches, and boots. He was allotted a bed in the state-room, near the fire, as he was sick. The next morning the vessel set sail, but afterwards ran aground opposite to Tilbury Point, where she remained about eight or ten days, and we did not get clear of the Thames for a fortnight. During all that time the passenger remained on board, except one day that he, along with the master of the vessel and my wife and I, went on shore, and dined at a neighbouring village, and another day that he went ashore by himself to get a bottle of milk.

For the first two or three days after the passenger came on board we called him 'the gentleman' as we did not know his name, but, upon my inquiring of him what his name was, he said it was John Dixon. [*Here Geddes identified Brodie as the man who called himself Dixon, as well as the letters that he had received from the prisoner and delivered to the sheriff. The key issue now became recognition – or not – of their handwriting and authenticity.*]

Robert Smith, wright in Edinburgh: I was some time ago foreman to the accused, Mr Brodie, and I remember to have been sent for by him upon the Sunday morning, the 9th of March, at eight o'clock, after it was reported that the Excise Office had been broke into. The message was not particular, but such a one as I usually received from him when he wanted to give me orders about some work, as he frequently sent for me for that purpose, especially if he was going to the country. When I came to him he asked me if there were any news about the people who had broke into the Excise. I answered that I had been informed that George Smith was committed to prison, and that Brown had been sent into England in search of Inglis & Homer's goods. I added that I hoped he, Mr Brodie, had no concern in these depredations; but he returned to me no answer.

The reason I asked this question was that I had often seen my master in their company, and knew him to be intimate with them. Mr Brodie told me he was going out of town for a few days, and sent me a message for a waistcoat and pair of breeches; but before my return he was gone, and I did not see him again till after he was brought back to this country. On the Monday evening following, the 10th of March, a search was made for him, and several doors of his house were broken open, in virtue of a warrant from the Sheriff, as I was informed. [*Here Smith was shown two letters referred to in the indictment, and asked if they were in Brodie's handwriting.*] I have seen the handwriting of Mr Brodie, and I think the writing of these letters very like his, but I never saw Mr Brodie subscribe with initials; and as I am no judge of writing, I cannot say whether I believe these letters to be written by Mr Brodie or not ...

James Laing, writer in Edinburgh: I am assistant clerk in the Council Chamber. I know Mr Brodie, the prisoner at the bar. I have seen him write, and I am a little acquainted with his handwriting. [*Here the two letters were shown.*] The writing of these letters is very like Mr Brodie's handwriting. I think they have been wrote by him. [*Here the unsigned scrolls were shown.*] I think these are of Mr Brodie's handwriting too, though worse written. [*State of affairs shown.*] I think this also is written by Mr Brodie.

John Macleish, clerk to Hugh Buchan, City Chamberlain of Edinburgh: I know Mr Brodie, the prisoner at the bar, and have had some opportunity of knowing his handwriting. I have got receipts from him in the Chamberlain's office, and have received cards from him. I have likewise seen him write in his own shop. [*Shown the two letters.*] I think these letters are of his handwriting. [*Shown the scrolls.*] I never saw Mr Brodie write in so crowded a way, or interline so much, but, notwithstanding, I think that these are of his handwriting.

Erskine – How do you come to know Mr Brodie's writing so exactly?

Macleish – From many accounts and receipts, of his writing, which I have in my custody belonging to the office.

With his handwriting generally recognised – and that being particularly relevant to the slipped-out admission of guilt in the main charge before the court – there was no apparent escape route for William Brodie, a position confirmed by the Lord Advocate's concluding, robust address to the jury.

After acknowledging that the letters Brodie gave to Geddes on board ship were 'strong' material, the Lord Advocate Islay Campbell said:

The other letters, or scrolls, found in his trunk are still stronger. You have had it clearly proven that all these letters are of his own handwriting, and in both of the scrolls he expressly acknowledges the crime for which he now stands at the bar. In one of them he says that he had no 'direct' concern in any of the late depredations of Smith, Brown, and Ainslie, excepting 'the last fatal one'; in the other the word 'direct' is scored out, but in both he acknowledges his accession to the last act; by which he can mean no other than the robbery of the Excise Office; for it happened on the Wednesday evening, and Brown gave information of it on the Friday evening immediately after. It was, therefore, in all probability the last of the depredations of this dangerous combination; and Mr Brodie's having applied the expression 'fatal' to it identifies it beyond all doubt …

I would, in the next place, gentlemen, have you to attend to the prisoner's behaviour when he flies from this place to London. He secretes himself in London for several weeks; search is made for him, but he cannot be found; he admits in one of his letters that he knew that Mr Williamson was in search of him, but he did not choose an interview; a vessel is freighted for him by some persons, contrary to the duty they owed to their country; she is cleared out for Leith; he goes on board of her in the middle of the night, with a wig on, in disguise, and under a borrowed name; he is carried to Flushing; he changes his name to John Dixon, and writes letters to people in Edinburgh under that false signature, explaining his whole future operations, in consequence of which letters he is traced and apprehended, just when he is on the point of going on board of a ship for New York …

Gentlemen, I beg leave now to bring under your consideration what happened in this city after Mr Brodie absconded. You have it in evidence that his house was searched, and various articles of a very suspicious nature found. A pair of pistols, identified to have been used on the occasion of the robbery, is found under the earth, and the place where they were hid pointed out by the other prisoner Smith; also a dark lanthorn, the one half of it in one place and the other half of it in another. Gentlemen, if Mr Brodie is really innocent, it appears to me passing strange that these articles should have been so concealed.

All these circumstances, gentlemen, are established by the most unexceptionable evidence; they are connected with and corroborated by each other; and they all point to this conclusion, independent altogether of the direct evidence of Brown and Ainslie: that Mr Brodie is guilty of the crime charged. They cannot be accounted for upon any other supposition.

Brodie was surely done for at this moment, and there was a detectable expression of alarm in his until now remarkably calm visage.

Did even he, convinced as he was of his own indestructability, see that the final dark curtain was coming down on his life?

And yet ... there was to be one more a dramatic development in the defence case and it was to come from an unexpected quarter: Smith's defence. Up to this point Brodie's miserable co-accused had had not a word spoken to help him. No witnesses had been called on his behalf, although he had been given two young counsel, advocates Robert Hamilton and John Clerk.

Much to the surprise of everyone who thought the respected and clever Dean of Faculty Henry Erskine would pull a last-minute rabbit out of the hat to save Brodie's skin, it was Clerk – a man with very little courtroom practice under his belt but with a lean and hungry look under the glasses he wore habitually on his brow – who would create a sensation in court and consequently give both the accused some new hope.

Concluding Fireworks

The most relevant witnesses at this juncture were those who saw the young John Clerk drink an entire bottle of claret with the object of putting himself, as he later phrased it, in 'fighting form'. He also said later that the exchanges that were to follow had been 'the making of me' – and they certainly provided the controversial launch pad for a celebrated career at the bar for the man who was to become Lord Eldin.

At this moment, however, he was still a junior partner in the defence team who had been at the bar less than three years and, while this was the most important case in which he had been employed and his first appearance in the Justiciary Court, he was determined to make a name for himself.

His senior colleague had probably not been aware of that. On the assumption that Erskine's plea on Brodie's behalf would be the more powerful address to the jury and leave the more lasting impact, he and Clerk had decided between themselves that the supporting act (the latter on behalf of Smith) would take the stage first.

The remarkable energy with which the fiery young counsel conducted his client's defence not only took Erskine aback but appalled all five judges on the bench, especially the broad-shouldered and broad-accented Lord Braxfield, who had never been spoken to like this in his life. Like what? Some exchanges between him and Clerk follow.

It has to be said, however, that although Clerk's comments prompted unheard-of sympathetic reactions among the public in court, and although his style was refreshingly audacious and even outrageous, later reflections of distinguished legal brains would say it was probably counter-productive; that Smith's cause (and incidentally Brodie's) might have been better served by a more temperate approach; that in the end Clerk had been – in Braxfield's words in the heat of battle – 'talking nonsense'.

But what exhilarating nonsense! The scene, which would seem incredible in modern courtrooms, began when the irrepressible young counsel came to deal with the admissibility of the evidence of the 'infernal scoundrels' Ainslie and Brown, and told the jury that these witnesses ought never to have been admitted:

Clerk – My unfortunate client is a very poor man ... an Englishman, a stranger in this country, and in great straits for his life, and whatever is favourable in his character or conduct is unknown; while, on the other hand, everything that tended to blacken his character and fix guilt upon him has been brought forward. He has no one to say a good word for him ... But, I, as his most inexperienced and imperfect counsel, will try and do the best I can for the poor man.

Braxfield – Be short and concise, sir, at this time of the morning.

Clerk – Pray, your Lordship, let me proceed.

Braxfield – Well then, proceed, young man.

Clerk – I come next to the testimony of Ainslie and Brown. Gentlemen, you have heard a variety of objections stated to the admissibility of their evidence – all of which has been overruled by the court. But notwithstanding the judgment of their Lordships, I must adhere to these objections and maintain that they ought not to have been admitted as witnesses. I think a great deal of most improper evidence has been received in this case for the Crown.

Braxfield – Do you say that, sir, after the judgment which the court has pronounced! That, sir, is a most improper observation to address at the outset to the jury.

Lord Stonefield – It is a positive reflection on the Court.

Lord Hailes – It is a flat accusation that we have admitted improper evidence.

Lord Eskgrove – I never heard the like of this from any young counsel at the beginning of his career at this bar.

Braxfield – With these admonitions, go on, sir; proceed, sir.

Clerk – Aweel, my Lords, if I go on, I beg to assail at the outset the evidence of these two corbies or infernal scoundrels, Ainslie and Brown.

Braxfield – Take care, sir, what you say.

Clerk – Yes, my Lords, I say that they are both most infamous characters. Gentlemen, you should discard such vagabonds, and not rely on their evidence in any way; and if you knock out the vile brains of their evidence in this case, there is nothing else remaining on which you can convict my poor client, except his own very candid declarations which I have already explained to you. Gentlemen, these nefarious witnesses Ainslie and Brown, should have stood at this bar this night in place of my client … Ainslie contradicts himself, and Brown is not to be believed. With respect to this said Mr John Brown, you had it out of his own mouth that he was a convicted felon in England, and I say to you that no convicted felon ought, by the good and glorious law of Scotland, to be received as a witness in this or any other case in the British dominions. [*Great applause from the public.*]

Macers – Silence in court.

Braxfield – Mr Clerk, please restrict your reflections. The court have admitted the witness.

Clerk – Yes, my Lords, I know that very well, but your Lordships should not have admitted him, and of that the jury will now judge.

Braxfield – This is most indecent behaviour. You cannot be allowed to speak to the admissibility; to the credibility you may.

Lord Stonefield – This young man is again attacking the court.

Clerk – No, my Lords, I am not attacking the court; I am attacking that villain of a witness, who, I tell your Lordships, is not worth his value in hemp.

Braxfield – The court, sir, have already solemnly decided, as you know, on the objections raised by Henry Erskine, that in law the objections to these witnesses should be repelled, and they were repelled accordingly; therefore you should have nothing more to say to us on that point.

Clerk – But, my Lords, the jury are to judge of the law as well as the facts.

Braxfield – Sir, I tell you that the jury have nothing to do with the law, but to take it simpliciter from me.

Clerk – That I deny. [*Consternation in court.*]

Lord Hailes – Sir, will you deny the authority of this High Court?

Clerk – Gentlemen of the jury, notwithstanding of this interruption, I beg to tell you, with all confidence and all respect, that you are the judges of the law as well as the facts. You are the judges of the whole case.

Braxfield – You are talking nonsense, sir.

Clerk – My Lord, you had better not snub me in this way. I never mean to speak nonsense.

Braxfield – Proceed – gang on, sir.

Clerk – Gentlemen, I was telling you that this infernal witness was convicted of felony in England, and how dare he come here to be received as a witness in this case?

Lord Advocate – He has, as I have shown you, received His Majesty's free pardon.

Clerk – Yes, I see; but, gentlemen of the jury, I ask you, on your oaths, can His Majesty make a tainted scoundrel an honest man? [*Applause in court.*]

Braxfield – Macers, clear the court if there is any more unruly din.

Lord Advocate [*addressing Mr Clerk*] – Sir, permit me to say, after this interruption, that the prerogative of mercy is the brightest jewel in His Majesty's Crown.

Clerk – I hope His Majesty's Crown will never be contaminated by any villains around it. [*Gasps of sensation in court.*]

Braxfield [*to Lord Advocate*] – Do you want his words noted down?

Lord Advocate – Oh no, my Lord, not exactly yet. My young friend will soon cool in his effervescence for his client.

Braxfield [*to Mr Clerk*] – Go on, young man.

Clerk – Gentlemen of the jury, I was just saying to you, when this outbreak on the bench occurred, that you were the judges of the law and of the facts in this case.

Braxfield – We cannot tolerate this, sir. It is an indignity to this High Court – a very gross indignity, deserving of the severest reprobation.

Clerk – My Lords, I know that your Lordships have determined this question; but the jury have not. They are judges both of fact and of the law, and are not bound by your Lordships' determination, unless it agrees with their own opinion. Unless I am allowed to speak to the jury in this manner, I am determined not to speak a word more. I am willing to sit down if your Lordships command me. [*Here he sat down.*]

Braxfield – Go on, sir; go on to the length of your tether.

Clerk – Yes, gentlemen, I stand up here as an independent Scottish advocate, and I tell you, a jury of my countrymen, that you are the judges of the law as well as of the facts.

Braxfield – Beware of what you are about, sir. [*Here he sat down again.*]

Lord Braxfield – Are you done, sir, with your speech?

Mr Clerk – No, my Lord, I am not.

Braxfield – Then go on, sir, at your peril.

Lord Hailes – You had better go on, Mr Clerk. Do go on.

Clerk – This has been too often repeated. I have met with no politeness from the court. You have interrupted me, you have snubbed me rather too often, my Lord, in the line of my defence. I maintain that the jury are judges of the law as well as of the facts; and I am positively resolved that I will proceed no further unless I am allowed to speak in my own way.

It was at this point that Clerk's most passionate outburst left everyone in court – especially Braxfield – open-mouthed with amazement. The judge sought to break the impasse by ordering that 'we must now call upon the Dean of Faculty to proceed with his address for the prisoner Brodie, which the court will hear with the greatest attention'. But Erskine seemed to decline the invitation, shaking his head negatively. What? Another mutineer? Braxfield had had enough. He would simply omit that stage. 'Very well,' he said, 'the court will now proceed and discharge its duty' – by which he meant he would now address the jury in his final charge. It was the provocation that sparked Clerk's now-famous explosion, as he jumped to his feet, shaking his fist at the bench:

Hang my client if you dare, my Lord, without hearing me in his defence!

This sensational moment stunned the court. While the public cheered and applauded, all the main players looked at each other in wide-eyed astonishment. There was nothing for it but to suspend proceedings. And when the judges retired to the robing room to hold an urgent consultation, there was general expectation that on their return there would be some sort of formal chastisement at least for the daring young counsel.

In the event, however, the wise old heads found a common strategy that rose no further to the young man's bait, and Clerk was allowed to proceed without interruption. And this he did, raising point after practical point in Smith's defence, while also making sure he had not entirely upstaged his senior colleague: 'Gentlemen, before I was interrupted, I was going to observe that in this branch of the evidence my cause is the same with that which is to be supported with so much greater abilities by Henry Erskine ...' and concluding that 'there has not been adduced on this trial sufficient legal evidence to warrant a verdict against Mr Smith'.

Indeed, Erskine's 7,500-word address to the jury at 3 a.m. was as thoroughly competent as had been expected, described as 'a fine example of forensic oratory', and also touched – more delicately – on the admissibility issue:

> You have on the one side a direct and positive proof of alibi which, if the witnesses are not foresworn, must preclude the possibility of the prisoner's guilt; and that these witnesses have departed from the truth there is not the shadow of reason to suspect. On the other hand, the whole direct evidence against the prisoner is the testimony of two witnesses who, besides being destitute of all right to be believed as witnesses in any case, have been brought to give evidence in the present in circumstances of the very strongest temptation to convict my unhappy client whether innocent or guilty, as but for their having accused him, one or both of them must have stood at his bar in his place.

But if the lords had avoided more confrontation by backing off from the battle, they had not on by any means conceded the war. In his final address to the jury, Lord Braxfield – still alert at 4.30 a.m. – was determined to win it, with surprisingly sensitive language, describing the crime in question as 'the most hurtful to society' and expressing distress at the situation of the prisoners – 'particularly one of them'. He had known Brodie's father as 'a very respectable man, and that the son – himself, too, educated to a respectable profession – should be arraigned at this bar for a crime so detestable, is what must affect us all, gentlemen, with sensations of horror'.

He continued:

That the Excise Office was broke into is not disputed. The question therefore is, who broke into it? Was it the prisoners? Now, to ascertain this point you have, in the first place, gentlemen, the evidence of Brown and Ainslie, and if they have sworn truth the prisoners must be guilty. To the admissibility of these witnesses there can be no objection. Were not evidence of this sort admissible, there would not be a possibility of detecting any crime of an occult nature. Had a corrupt bargain, indeed, been proved, by which they were induced to give their evidence, there might have been room for an objection to their admissibility. But no such bargain has even been alleged against the public prosecutor in the present case. And as to their being accomplices, this, gentlemen, is no objection at all. A proof by accomplices may display, it is true, a corruption of manners, which alone can render such proof necessary. But it is impossible to go into the idea that their testimony is therefore inadmissible.

Nor is there, in the present case, any reason to suppose that they were under improper temptations to give their evidence. Each was separately called upon by the court, and it was explained to them that they ran no hazard unless from not speaking the truth, and that their being produced as witnesses secured them from all punishment, except what would follow upon their giving false evidence. Under such circumstances, you cannot suppose, gentlemen, that they would be guilty of perjury without any prospect of advantage to themselves, and merely to swear away the lives of these prisoners at the bar. Their credibility, to be sure, rests with you, gentlemen; and if you find anything unnatural or contradictory in their evidence you will reject it. But there is nothing in it unnatural or contradictory.

Upon the whole, gentlemen, taking all the circumstances of this case together, I can have no doubt in my own mind that Mr Brodie was present at the breaking into the Excise Office; and as to the other man. Smith, as I have already said, there can be still less doubt as to him. If you are of the same opinion, gentlemen, you will return a verdict against both the prisoners; but if you are of a different opinion, and do not consider the evidence against Brodie sufficiently strong, you will separate the one from the other, and bring in a verdict accordingly.

Braxfield ended his charge at six o'clock on Thursday morning, and the court adjourned until one o'clock in the afternoon – when the Chancellor of the jury handed in their written verdict, sealed with black wax, unanimously finding both prisoners guilty. The Lord Justice Clerk then addressed the prisoners thus:

William Brodie and George Smith, it belongs to my office to pronounce the sentence of the law against you. You have had a long and fair trial, conducted on the part of the public prosecutor with the utmost candour and humanity, and you have been assisted with able counsel, who have exerted the greatest ability and fidelity in your defence.

I wish I could be of any use to you in your melancholy situation. To one of you it is altogether needless for me to offer any advice. You, William Brodie, from your education and habits of life, cannot but know everything suited to your present situation which I could suggest. It is much to be lamented that those vices, which are called gentlemanly vices, are so favourably looked upon in the present age. They have been the source of your ruin … I hope you will improve in the short time you have now to live by reflecting upon your past conduct and endeavouring to procure, by a sincere repentance, forgiveness for your many crimes. God always listens to those who seek Him with sincerity.

Braxfield then pronounced sentence of death, requiring:

The prisoners William Brodie and George Smith to be carried from the bar back to the Tolbooth of Edinburgh, therein to be detained till Wednesday, the first day of October next, and upon that day to be taken furth of the said Tolbooth to the place fixed upon by the magistrates of Edinburgh as a common place of execution, and then and there, betwixt the hours of two and four o'clock afternoon to be hanged by the necks, by the hands of the Common Executioner, upon a gibbet, until they be dead; and ordain all their moveable goods and gear to be escheat and inbrought to His Majesty's use: which is pronounced for doom.

How did they take it? A contemporary account said: 'Mr Brodie discovered some inclination to address himself to the court, but when restrained by his counsel contented himself with bowing to the bench.' Aeneas Morrison, the agent for Smith, reported:

> The prisoners behaved in a manner different from each other, Smith appearing to be much dejected, especially at receiving his dreadful sentence …
>
> Mr Brodie, on the other hand, affected coolness and determination in his behaviour. When the sentence of death was pronounced he put one hand in his breast and the other in his side and looked full around him. It is said that he accused his companion of pusillanimity, and even kicked him as they were leaving the court. Thus ended a trial which had excited the public curiosity to an extraordinary degree, and in which their expectations were not disappointed. During the space of twenty-one hours – the time it lasted – circumstances continually followed each other to render it highly interesting, and more particularly to the gentlemen of the law, on account of the great variety and importance of the legal topics which were discussed and decided.

When the court rose and the prisoners were removed to the Tolbooth, escorted by the City Guard amid a huge crowd of spectators, William Brodie was seen to have a strange smirk on his face.

What did he now have up his lacy-cuffed sleeve?

7

DEATH (OR NOT?)
BY HANGING

'Fare ye well, Bailie! You needn't be surprised if ye see me among
ye yet, to take my share of the deid-chack!'

*The 'deid-chack' was a meal enjoyed by the provost and council after an
execution, and this valedictory (or not) message was spoken out by a surprisingly optimistic Deacon Brodie as he prepared to meet his maker (or not).*

The truths, half-truths and outright fabrications that persist today
regarding Deacon Brodie's dramatic demise had begun to take
root even before he stepped up to the gallows on the first day of
October 1788. He was already a less-than-admired legend in his
lifetime, though that life was about to be cut short at the age of 47.
Or was it? Feeding the many stories about the end, or not, of this
diminutive but larger-than-life character was his strangely relaxed
and almost arrogant attitude towards the final curtain. A huge crowd
of around 40,000 had gathered to witness the spectacle before
his jailhouse, the dilapidated fourteenth-century Old Tolbooth,
a stone's throw from his Lawnmarket workshop and home; to many
of them something about his easy demeanour suggested he did
not believe the curtain was really going to fall. Perhaps it was just

his final defence mechanism, a what-the-hell denial in the face of such a momentous prospect or – more likely – there was something more complex and cunning going on inside the scheming brain of this man, who had always believed he was one of life's survivors.

Was he one of death's survivors too? Could he really cheat the hangman's rope? The most common scandalous tale that has lived on was that he engaged a surgeon to fashion a steel tube to fit inside or – more likely – around his throat and protect it from the squeezing of the rope during the 'fatal' drop ... and that the executioner had been bribed not to notice the odd bulge around his neck. Indeed, the Deacon was seen to converse with the hangman several times at the scaffold while having the rope's length adjusted, this apparently with a professional eye, as the skilled cabinet-maker was said to have been instrumental in the previous year's redesign of the awful apparatus, whose old-school ladders had been replaced by a clever mechanism – irony of ironies, if true!

Probably not true, however. The neck-protection theory was itself hanged over time, though the idea of some collusion with the executioner was never quite written off. But Brodie's part in the death-dealing redesign, a tale probably generated by irony-loving romantics, was later relegated to 'probably minimal' by less gullible and more serious academic types such as William Roughhead, the Scottish lawyer, editor and essayist on 'matters criminous'. He wrote in his *Classic Crimes* that, after considerable research, he was sure that although the Deacon may have had some hand in the design, the new concept 'was certainly not of his construction, nor was he the first to benefit by its ingenuity'.

But if Brodie were not so familiar with the new gallows as suspected by some who believed he knew how to manipulate its workings to his advantage, and if the metal windpipe theory was too incredible, what would explain the condemned man's quiet confidence in the face of his impending doom? What was going on?

Another, largely true local story might have had a significant bearing on his bearing, as it were. Some sixty years earlier, fish-hawker Maggie Dickson had been publicly hanged in the Grassmarket for killing her unwanted baby whose father was not her absent husband – but despite being pronounced dead on her parting from the noose, she survived due to a combination of circumstances. These were her relatively youthful health, those earlier not-so efficient gallows and a rough cart ride part of the six-mile way to Musselburgh, during which, to her friends' astonishment, she started banging, shouting and knocking from inside her wooden coffin. Seen to be very much alive on the lifting of the lid, she then enjoyed unusual leniency from the law – which, believing her survival to be God's will, declared her officially free.

Some cynics said she had used her feminine wiles to have the ropemaker weaken the noose – and used them also to win over the forgiveness of the law officers, though it was clear that luck had been very much on her side. Not to mention the shrugged shoulders of fate, for in some enlightened cultures it was held by common consent, though never actually by law, that it was permissible to remove a hanged person from the foot of the gallows and attempt to revive them; so that if they survived they were morally entitled to go free. Such attempts sometimes succeeded, but they were often thwarted by the density and interference of the thronging crowds.

In any case, 'Half Hangit Maggie', as Miss Dickson then became half-affectionately called by the locals, became something of a community character as she had two more children – by her husband – and lived on for another forty years, moving awkwardly around the city with her head permanently locked over to one side.

Brodie was doubtless only too familiar with the saga of her salvation and he surely took heart from it as he contemplated his fate. Could he too pull that one off? One persistent story was that he had made an arrangement with an Edinburgh-resident French doctor, Pierre Degravers (who claimed to have been 'Professor of Anatomy and Physiology in the Royal Academy of Science' in Paris) – the same man perhaps who didn't stick his neck out to save

Brodie's with a metal throat-tube? – after a 'consultation' with him in his Old Tollbooth cell on a day close to his date with destiny. And if Brodie's life prospects were looking pretty grim, his living conditions were even grimmer; so it would have surprised few if intolerance of his rat-infested existence had moved him to a last request for treatment for depression.

But in the thirty-four days between his trial beginning in late August 1788 and his early October rendezvous with the scaffold, he somehow managed to keep up his spirits by dressing well despite being in chains, singing extracts from *The Beggars' Opera* and playing draughts with himself and any interested visitors – after cutting out a rough draughtboard on the stone floor of his dungeon.

That craftwork was said to have been still in place when the crumbling old building was demolished – along with the adjoining block of shops and residential tenement buildings known as 'the Luckenbooths' – in 1817. And not before time. In an era that had no concern for conservation of historic architecture, their destruction had been desired by the populace for literally centuries. Why? Since coming into being, the buildings were considered an 'ugly encumbrance and deformity to the High Street', causing an unwanted obstruction and inhibiting flow of people, horses, carts and sedan chairs in the centre of the High Street to a narrow passage only 14ft wide in places. But that was only one of its negative points.

Although it can look medievally handsome today in old prints, the Old Tollbooth had long been a little-loved edifice among Brodie's fellow Edinburghers and their forebears and – by any technical assessment – should have been knocked down long before its fourth century, when Brodie was forced to regard it as his second home on the High Street. Today its one-time existence is marked by a heart shape made of cobbles – 'the heart of Midlothian' – and the locals' tourist-shocking modern habit of spitting on it is probably more than the good-luck gesture they believe it to be; it no doubt dates back to the time when the building was held in total disdain for several reasons.

To compound the ghastliness of the sky-high house of horrors, its exterior had provided the blood-curdling stage for judicial torture and executions. The gallows were attached to the west gable on a protruding platform high enough to give rubber-necking spectators the most open view of the gory proceedings. And on the upper reaches of the jail's walls rusty old spikes were fixed into the mossy stone to facilitate display of the various body parts of those punished with the heaviest penalties. Such as the head of the Charles I loyalist hero James Graham, 1st Marquis of Montrose, which was exhibited there for over ten years from 1650 to 1661, after he was deserted by Charles II and hanged at the Mercat Cross.

Having grown out of its various earlier purposes – as a toll collection booth, a centre where the city's trading regulations would be sorted out by merchants, a meeting place of the town councillors and the grudging venue for the white-wigged grumblers of the Court of Session – it was eventually rejected by all its users in favour of what had become its primary purpose: the incarceration and brutal treatment of thieves, rogues and murderers in unimaginably squalid conditions. They would be chained by one leg to an iron bar, along which they could minimally walk (though Brodie was allowed a longer chain than was regular, as well as pen and ink, and occasional visits from friends).

Many such prisoners would be held here before being executed or, if lucky, transported off to work on the American plantations. And by the time Brodie was keen to get away, to anywhere at all that was not the scaffold, the now independent Americans had closed the door – while a new one had opened at Australia's Botany Bay, discovered nearly two decades before by Captain Cook. With that escape route in mind, the Deacon had another couple of cards up his sleeve. But time was tight. With only two weeks left to live, he wrote appealingly to a pair of very important persons in the vain hope that their influence could, even at this late stage, change the course of his court-decided fate. Datelined the Tolbooth, 10 September 1788, the first letter was to the Right Hon Henry Dundas (Viscount Melville) and it read:

Right Honble, Sir

You are no doubt acquainted with my misfortunes. Extracts of the proceedings against me are sent to London by my friends to endeavour to procure a Remission or an Alteration of my Sentence. But I believe little respect is paid to such Aplications unless supported by respectable Personages. With which view I now most humbly beseech your interposition and interest in support of this application making in London in my behalf and if possible prevent me from suffering an Ignomnious Death to the disgrace of my numerous conections, even if it were to end my days at Bottony Bay.

As the time appointed for my Disolution approaches fast, I most earnestly intreat no time may be lost in writing to London on my behalf.

I now most humbly Beg that you will pardon this Presumption in one of the most unfortunate of the Human Race and whatever may be the result of this Aplication, I shall ever pray for your welfare and happiness.

I am with the greatest respect Right Honble Sir

Your most obdt and huble Sert but most unfortunate

Will Brodie

The second letter, with the same dateline, was to Her Grace the Duchess of Buccleuch, and read:

Madam,

Lett me beseech your Ladyship to pardon My Boldness in making the present address.

The wretched can only fly to the Humane and the powerfull for Relief. As my triall is printed, it would ill suit me to make any reflections on the unfortunate Issue; and this much I am convinced of, that the Current of Popular prejudice is so strong against me, that it will be well with me if I can Rescue my Life on any terms; and though my friends are making aplication above, I have little hopes of the success, unless some Respectable Characters who have had an opportunity of knowing something of those I have come of, and of my former life, Interest themselves in my behalf.

With all the fortitude of a man, I must confess to you, Madam, that I feel the Natural horror at Death, and particularly a violent Ignominious Death, and would willingly avoid it even on the condition of spending my Future years at Bottony Bay.

In that Infant Collony I might be usefull, from my knowledge in several Mechanical branches beside my own particular Profession; and if your Ladyship and your most Respectable friend The Right Honble Henry Dundas, would Deign to Patronise my Suit, I would have little Reason to Doubt the Success. Capt John Hamilton too I think would be ready to assist in any measure Sanctified by your Ladyship.

Lett me again intreat you to Pardon my Boldness. My time flies apace, and the hand of Death presses upon me. Think for one moment, but no longer, what it is to be wretched, doomed to Death, helpless and in Chains, and you will excuse an effort for life from the most Infatuated and miserable of Men, who can confer no Compliment insubscribing Himself.

Madam,
Your Ladyships Devoted
Huble Sert
Will:m Brodie

To stress the misery of his situation, he added to his sign-off: 'Edinr Tolbooth in the Iron Room and in Chains'. But even without such a note, it was obvious that, all in all, the Old Tolbooth was not a wonderfully cheering spot in which to spend your last days and hours while fighting off depression, especially while the clock ticked on inexorably and the ensuing silence spoke loudly of the futility of appeals.

What of the good French doctor, then? His visit to this forbidding place – if it happened at all – was said to have concerned more body than mind or soul. It was reported that he had undertaken, presumably for a good price, to revive Brodie after his body's release from the rope and that, to effect helpful bleeding, he had pencil-marked the condemned man's arms and temples to indicate where he would make the cuts.

It is tempting to conclude that Brodie's puzzlingly relaxed manner on the scaffold in defiance of his bleak future had something to do with such an apparently reassuring strategy, though this unexpected behaviour at that critical juncture may also have reflected his perverse enjoyment of the limelight after all these dark days lurking and hiding from people down damp, pitch-black closes with only fearful accomplices and a small flickering lantern to relieve the gloom.

So where was his big farewell speech to the thousands of onlookers? Such an egotist would surely have wanted to speak out boldly (yet humbly) in his own defence and take his leave with something of a swagger. The absence of such a piece of theatre seemed to confirm that he intended to return from his appointment with the Grim Reaper.

The nearest he got to that kind of showing off was when – just before pulling the nightcap over his face – he took a nearby friend by the hand, bade him farewell and requested that he acquaint the world with the view that he was still the same and that he died like a man.

To other friends whom he had seen more privately that morning, he had seemed remarkably self-possessed, cool, contained and almost indifferent to his fate, speaking of it light-heartedly as 'a leap in the dark'. He had shown real emotion only when visited, for the last time, by his pretty 10-year-old daughter Cecill on the Friday before his execution, 'and here nature and the feelings of a father were superior to every other consideration; and the falling tear which he endeavoured to suppress gave strong proofs of his sensibility – he embraced her with emotion and blessed her with the warmest affection'. That observation was courtesy of *The Scots Magazine*, an extract from the first of two contemporary accounts, reprinted below, that described the dramatic moments and circumstances around the execution of Brodie and his accomplice George Smith:

When Mr Brodie came to the scaffold, he bowed politely to the magistrates and the people. He had on a full suit of black – his hair dressed and powdered. Smith was dressed in white linen, trimmed with black. Having spent some time in prayer, with seeming fervency, with the clergymen, Mr Brodie then prayed a short time by himself.

Having put on white nightcaps, Brodie pointed to Smith to ascend the steps that led to the drop, and, in an easy manner, clapping him on the shoulder, said: 'George Smith, you are first in hand.' Upon this, Smith, whose behaviour was highly penitent and resigned, slowly ascended the steps and was immediately followed by Brodie, who mounted with briskness and agility, and examined the dreadful apparatus with attention, and particularly the halter designed for himself. The ropes being too short-tied, Brodie stepped down to the platform and entered into conversation with his friends. He then sprang up again but the rope was still too short; and he once more descended to the platform showing some impatience.

During this dreadful interval Smith remained on the drop with great composure and placidness. Brodie having ascended a third time, and the rope being at last properly adjusted, he deliberately untied his neckcloth, buttoned up his waistcoat and coat, and helped the executioner to fix the rope. He then pulled the nightcap over his face and placed himself in an attitude expressive of firmness and resolution.

Smith, who during all this time had been in fervent devotion, let fall a handkerchief as a signal, and a few minutes before three they were launched into eternity, almost without a struggle.

Brodie on the scaffold neither confessed nor denied his being guilty, and the justice of his sentence, and showed in all his conduct proper expressions of penitence, humility, and faith. Smith, with great fervency, confided in prayer his being guilty, and the justice of his sentence, and showed in all his conduct the proper expressions of penitence, humility, and faith.

'This execution was conducted with more than usual solemnity; and the great bell tolled during the ceremony, which had an awful and solemn effect. The crowd of spectators was immense.

Considering his long-term antipathy towards Brodie, juryman William Creech's report of the hanging – published within days and within his *Account of the Trial of William Brodie and George Smith* – might not have been entirely objective; indeed it was nuanced with a touch of *Schadenfreude*, though it also gave an occasionally sympathetic summing up of the raw atmosphere that prevailed among key characters at the time, beginning as it did with the condemned man's trying days in the Old Tolbooth jail before the big event:

On the Sunday preceding his execution a respite of six weeks arrived for Falconer and Bruce [fellow-prisoners condemned for robbing a Dundee Bank]. The news made Brodie more serious for a little time than he had before been, and he expressed his satisfaction at the event. – Smith said, six weeks is but a short period. Brodie, with emotion answered, George, What would you and I give for six weeks longer? Six weeks would be an age to us.

On Tuesday morning, the day before his execution, a gentleman who was visiting him occasionally remarked on the fatal conse-quences of being connected with bad women, and in how many instances it had proved ruinous. – Yes, said Brodie, 'Tis woman that seduces all mankind [from *The Beggars' Opera*]. The gentleman reproved this levity; but he sung out the song:

'Tis woman that seduces all mankind
By her we first were taught the wheedling arts
Her very Eyes can cheat; when most she's kind,
She tricks us ...

On the Tuesday evening, the 30th of September, the Magistrates gave an order that none should be admitted to him but clergy-men: A report having prevailed that there was an intention of putting self-destruction in his power. But of this order he com-plained, and declared that, if poison was placed on one hand, and a dagger at the other, he would refuse them both – he would submit to the sentence of the laws of his country. Late in the evening he was suddenly agitated by hearing some noise; and turning to Smith, he said – George, do you know what that noise is? No, said Smith – Then I'll tell you. It is the drawing out of the fatal beam on which you and I must suffer tomorrow – I know it well.

Soon after eleven he went to bed, and slept till four in the morning, and continued in bed till near eight. At nine (Wednesday, October 1.) he had his hair fully dressed and powdered. Soon after, a clergyman entered, and offered to pray with him. He desired that it might be as short as possible. At eleven o'clock he wrote the following letter to the Lord Provost in a strong, firm hand:

> *Edinburgh, Tolbooth,*
> *Oct 1. 1788, Eleven o'clock.*
>
> *My Lord*
>
> *As none of my relations can stand being present at my dissolution, I humbly request that your Lordship will permit [name deleted] to attend, it will be some consolation in my last hour; and that your Lordship will please give order that my body after be delivered to [name deleted] and by no means to remain in jail; that he and my friends may have it decently dressed and interred. This is the last favour and request of*
>
> *Your most obedient*
> *But most unfortunate*
> *[Signed] Will. Brodie*

Much to his relief, this request was granted, and he considered it one of the more humane acts he had encountered of late; it would certainly soften the blow that was about to fell him ... or not. Creech's account continued:

At about one o'clock he ate a beef-steak, and drank some port wine; and during this last repast he made some ludicrous remarks to Smith, &c.

At two o'clock the guard marched up and surrounded the place of execution; and soon after the Captain on duty informed the Magistrates in the Council Chamber that all was ready.

The Magistrates then put on their robes of office, with white gloves, and white slaves, and followed by the clergymen in black gowns and bands, proceeded from the Council Chamber to the prison, attended by the proper officers.

The Magistrates reached the scaffold at about ten minutes after two. The criminals were soon brought out –

Brodie, at the first view of the immense multitude of specta-tors, and the dreadful apparatus, said, This is awful! – On passing a gentleman he asked how he did, and said he was glad to see him. – The gentleman answered, he was sorry to see Mr Brodie in that situation. Brodie replied, It is *fortune de la guerre.*

Brodie had on a full suit of black, his hair dressed and powdered; Smith was dressed in white, with black trimming. They were assisted in their devotions by the Rev. Mr Hardie, one of the ministers of the city, the Rev. Mr Cleeve of the Episcopal, and Mr Hall of the Burgher persuasion. They spend some time in praying with seem-ing fervency. Brodie kneelt, laying a handkerchief under his knees. He prayed by himself, nearly as follows:

O Lord, I acknowledge thee as the Great Ruler of the world; although I lament much that I know so little of thee. This much, however, I know, that thou art a merciful God, and that, as I am a great sinner, thou wilt have mercy upon me, through the merits of they Son Jesus Christ! O Lord, receive my soul! Into they hands I resign it. Amen.

When the devotions were over, the great bell began to toll, at half-minute pauses, which had an awful and solemn effect. The criminals put on white caps, and Smith, whose behaviour was highly penitent and resigned, slowly ascended the platform, raised a few feet above the scaffold, and placed immediately under the beam where the halters were fixed …

[It was at this point that Brodie tapped his accomplice on the shoulder, saying, 'Go up, George, you are first in hand.']

He was followed by Brodie, who mounted with alertness and examined the dreadful apparatus with attention, particularly the halter designed for himself, which he pulled with his hand. It was found that the halters had been too much shortened and they were obliged to be taken down to alter.

Smith remained on the platform trembling, but Brodie stepped briskly down to the scaffold, took off his night-cap and again entered into conversation with his friends, till the ropes were adjusted. He then sprung up again upon the platform, but the rope was still improperly placed, and he once more descended, showing some little impatience, and observed, that the executioner was a bungling fellow and ought to be punished for his stupidity. – but that it did not much signify. Having again ascended, he deliberately untied his cravat, buttoned up his waistcoat and coat, and helped the executioner to fix the rope; then pulling the night-cap over his face, he folded his arms and placed himself in an attitude expressive of firmness and resolution.

Some aspects of the whole affair were so murky it was hardly surprising that rich conspiracy stories kept emerging and circulating – such as the widespread suspicion that the hangman had been bargained with to arrange for a short fall, thus the inordinate time spent fiddling with the rope. Thus also perhaps the showy condemnation of the man's 'stupidity' – to suggest that someone so maligned by Brodie could not possibly have been in league with him. In any case, 'the excess of caution exercised by the executioner, in the first instance, in shortening the rope, proved fatal by his inadvertency in making it latterly too long', observed one witness to the scene.

Creech went on:

Smith, (who during the interruption, had been in fervent devotion,) soon after the adjustment of the halters, let fall a handkerchief as a signal, and a few minutes before three the platform dropt, and they were launched into eternity.

Thus ended the life of William Brodie and of George Smith.

Brodie had neither confessed not denied the crimes for which he suffered. To a gentleman who visited him a day before his execution, he said, he thought it was hard to suffer so for such a paltry sum, and appealing to Smith, he said – George, it was not more than £4 apiece. – Smith answered that he did not think it was so much, but he, Brodie, should know, as he coveted the money.

The following elaboration is extracted from Robert Chalmers' *Traditions of Edinburgh*:

His dress and deportment at the gallows displayed a mind at ease, and gave some countenance to the popular notion that he had made certain mechanical arrangements for saving his life …

When placed on that insecure pedestal, and while the rope was adjusted around his neck by the executioner, his courage did not forsake him. On the contrary, even there he exhibited a sort of levity; he shuffled about, looked gaily around, and finally went out of the world with his hand stuck carelessly into the open front of his vest.

Or did he? Roughead reported that an early plan to rescue the Deacon – by overpowering the city and guard and breaking into the Tollbooth – had been abandoned by his friends in favour of a more sophisticated strategy; this was the one that now (allegedly) went into operation. When cut down, Brodie's body was handed over to two of his own workmen, who quickly placed it on a cart, and drove it at a full, bone-shaking pace round the back of the castle, presumably with the idea that such a rough ride might provoke resuscitation à la Maggie Dickson. That was not to be, but the corpse was then taken to one of Brodie's workshops in the Lawnmarket, where Dr Degravers was – reportedly – in attendance. However, all attempts at bleeding failed; Brodie had not been breathing for many long minutes and was finally pronounced to be 'fairly gone'.

The following footnote appeared in Creech's report of the affair: 'Much anxiety was shown that the body might not be detained in prison; and after the Magistrates retired a vein was opened. It is said other means of recovery were used after it was taken away, but the neck was found to be dislocated.'

All of which would sound decidedly terminal to any sensible person, so why – even when Brodie had (apparently) found his way to an unmarked grave at the Buccleuch Church in Chapel Street – was his termination unaccepted by so many sceptics? There was widespread local talk that, after a 'set-up' exit, a 'born-again' Brodie had found his way abroad. Some said he had fled to his original escape destination of New York; others swore he had been seen on the streets of Paris where he had taken up residence. *Pardon?* as they might say in the French capital. Roughead again: 'There is a tradition that, on a subsequent occasion, the grave was opened, when no trace of his body could be found.'

Had it then contained someone else? The theories still bubble on, well into the third century of Deacon Brodie's dark story, but there is little chance of doubts being settled now, as the burial ground is now covered by a car park behind university lecture halls.

But just for the fascination of it, let's think about this more than one-dimensionally. 'The neck was found to be dislocated' – who said that? If it is to be attributed to Dr Degravers, who would have been part of any getaway conspiracy, it is not a huge stretch of the imagination to respond: 'He would say that, wouldn't he?' It's what Edinburgh University's Owen Dudley Edwards calls his Mandy Rice-Davies theory (look it up) and as one who has written and broadcasted many thousands of words on the Brodie case, he feels there are many other areas of doubt about the 'death' that have never really been resolved.

Speaking over a black coffee in the stairwell café of the National Library of Scotland on George IV Bridge – not much more than

100m from the scene of the (punishment of the) crime – the distinguished historian and author of many academic books explains why he leans towards the theory that Brodie was indeed revived and removed from the scene of his 'death'. While conceding that there is no solid evidence for that belief, he feels that the middle-class miscreant 'was so well connected in Edinburgh society, with a circle of important business and political contacts and even genuine friends, that his fate would have been comprehensively protected by them when any official or reporter asked them or his doctor for confirmation of his demise'. In other words, the enquirers would have been sold a dummy or, to put it even more bluntly, told an outright lie.

'Let's face it,' says the historian, 'this could have been the idea from the start – for the cheating of the gallows to succeed, for friends to be primed to say he was gone, to feign grief, see off any questioners and, once the episode had blown over, to quietly help him out of the city and the country.'

Dudley Edwards thinks it likely that Brodie was hidden away for a while, provided with new identity and disguises, and 'smuggled to America' where he lived out his days. Indeed, the historian once memorably said so with persuasive conviction in a feature called *Case Reopened* on BBC Radio Scotland:

Brodie's excellent connections stretched to the judge himself at the trial, who was embarrassed he had known Brodie and, more importantly, 'kent his fether'. And let's not forget what a clever man this uncommon thief was. He would not have given up his life easily, that's for sure, and would have employed every possible means at his disposal to sustain it.

So I believe it's more than possible that he survived. The only evidence we have that he died are the statements to that effect from the people around him, but these were his own friends. They said he was dead but, frankly, that was not reliable evidence. You wouldn't expect them to say anything else. We know his friends put out a very odd story, that he had hoped to survive, but had failed. So basically, it was all very suspicious. It suggests they were anxious to prevent rumours that this is exactly what had happened.

Also, Brodie was not hanged for murder, so his body was not the property of the state and taken away for dissection. The historian also points to the fact that there is no direct evidence of a burial.

So how exactly could he have cheated the hangman, assuming there is doubt about the steel collar idea, but at the same time accepting that he was an expert in carpentry?

Whether or not he was hanged on a gibbet of his own design, as has been reported many times, he had been certainly involved to some degree of consultancy on its reconception the year before, so he understood the new workings.

He knew he ran the risk of being hanged and knew how he could have a good chance of avoiding it. The gibbet was reinforced so that it didn't break his neck on the first drop.

What had he been talking to the hangman about before he made the drop? Again, it does not stretch the imagination to think that there was some collusion there.

And if the rope was the right length he would be okay. There would have been a bit of a jar, but he had a plan and nothing would have been broken. Once supposedly hanged, he would plunge through a platform taking him out of sight.

The structure underneath the actual gallows was hidden away from the public. And Brodie's friends were there, immediately receiving the body, and he was almost certainly still alive. He would have been taken down very quickly and spirited away.

So resurrection is the definitive conclusion? 'It is at least as good a theory as any other, and I would say a good deal better,' says

Dudley Edwards with a mischievous twinkle, which prompts the listener to suspect he would find it rather a shame if the mystery were actually to be solved.

And wait … what is this we have here? Just to muddy the waters still further, we note that in its issue of 1823 – thirty-five years after the drama – *Blackwood's Edinburgh Magazine* had something to say about it in a series of 'imaginary colloquies' with a scenario attended by Timothy Tickler, Morgan O'Doherty, James Hogg and Christopher North (the fictitious editor, who was actually editor John Wilson) chairing the discussion in 'The Blue Room, crowded with bottles at 1 in the morning'. It seems Mr Tickler, a croupier to trade, claimed to have been a witness of the hanging and had not been impressed by the magazine's previous 'bad' number that had carried a piece on Mr Brodie and his fate:

> North: 'What was your chief objection?'
> Tickler: 'That shocking, that atrocious lie, about Brodie – or I should say, that bundle of lies.'
> O'Doherty: 'I wrote it.'
> Tickler: 'That paragraph was full of shocking misstatements. The fact is, I saw Brodie hanged and he had no silver tube in his windpipe, and no flowered waistcoat on. It is true that he sent for a doctor to ask if there was any probability of escaping with life, but [Pierre] Degravers told him at once, sir, that he would be "as dead as Julius Caesar"; these were the words. But Brodie would hold his own opinion; and nobody e'er threw down the pocket handkerchief more assured of resuscitation. Poor devil! He just spun round a few times and then hung there as quiet as you please with his pigtail looking up to heaven.'
> O'Doherty: 'Alas! Poor Brodie!'

Just how imaginary was that discussion? Not entirely, one has to suspect. There is a detectable authenticity about it, is there not? And so the mystery goes on.

Not just one mystery, actually. In many ways, the saga of the man with the double life is still riddled with a variety of puzzles. He had alluded to one of them himself (as reported in *The Scots Magazine*) on realising that he was facing the ultimate punishment for what he considered his minor crimes:

> He declared that, not withstanding the censures and opinions of the world, he was innocent of every crime except that for which he was condemned; and endeavoured to extenuate his guilt by saying that the crime for which he suffered was not a depradation committed on an individual, but on the public, who could not be injured by the small trifle the Excise was robbed of.

In other words, he may not have been the honest, upstanding citizen he pretended to be (at least by day) and perhaps he would venture out on one or two of his night jobs with a selection of deadly pistols, but he was still not a murderer, surely just a glorified burglar who hadn't won much for his troubles and who hadn't hurt anyone. Did that really merit the death sentence?

Maybe not, but another puzzle, for this writer at least, is the extent to which such a miscreant was and is let off the hook and celebrated, even in today's world. Most people in Scotland, and many much further afield, would claim at least to have heard of him, though they might not be familiar with the details of his story. There are several pubs that revel in the resonance of his name – from Dundee through his native Edinburgh to Chicago and the place where he once wanted to end up: New York.

As is mentioned elsewhere in this volume, the arched alleyway off Edinburgh's Lawnmarket that housed his home and workshops still boasts not just the Brodie's Close plaque above its entrance but a full-size replica of the man himself just outside, inviting passers-by into the restaurant within, which occupies the Deacon's one-time working space. Where once there was wood, now there is food.

There have been songs, plays and books written about him; in 1997 a television movie of the same name was made starring the Scottish actor-comedian Billy Connolly.

As observed in chapter 1, the even better-known split personality of Dr Jekyll and Mr Hyde that Deacon Brodie spawned through the vivid imagination of Robert Louis Stevenson has become even more internationally iconic, adapted for countless plays, movies and other channels of popular culture, while the very phrase has entered the English language as a kind of shorthand for someone who encapsulates good and evil.

The series of disturbing questions that this raises starts, of course, with 'Why do we allow it?' And it follows with 'Why are some villainous rogues almost forgiven as we elevate them – like Ned Kelly, Ronnie Biggs, Deacon Brodie – to a status that can even overtake that of the good-guy heroes?' and 'Why do we enjoy explorations of badness as much in real life as in dark thrillers? Is it because both good and evil are to be found in all of us and it is perhaps best that we indulge the latter characteristic vicariously, at arm's length, through the device of daredevil personalities, real or fictional?' Answer if you dare.

It was a theme that obviously fascinated Stevenson, who himself was given to dabbling in the two sides of his own personality, moving as he did between the extreme Victorian respectability of his parents' elegant New Town and the looser worlds that he relished, whether represented by the 'trivial lecheries' of Edinburgh's 'vicious lamp-lit fairyland' or the bohemian life he fled to – after rejecting the law career so desired by his family – among the mistressed, carefree company of art students in France.

He clearly believed everyone to be capable of a double life – and Dr Jekyll was surely his way of urging us to acknowledge this human trait that, he would say, varies among individuals only by degrees of intensity and controllability.

So in many ways the masked intruder who inspired that sinister creation did not really die here or even there; the man who was the original Jekyll and Hyde lives on not just in the ghostly shadows of old Edinburgh but in our own hearts, fears and imaginations.

The Family Bible

Whether or not the disgraced deacon lived on, it can't be denied that there was a clear desire among his surviving family to see his name removed as much as possible from evidence of his existence – so especially from the family Bible which accommodated, between the pages of its Old and New Testaments, a handwritten manuscript of many pages registering Brodie births, marriages and deaths.

It was the fondly maintained work of William's father Francis and began with his own birth in 1708, carrying on with that of his wife, Cicel Grant, in 1718, their marriage in 1740, and the births of their eleven children – most dying in their infancy – along with the deaths of other relatives.

One name whose birth and death no longer feature in these pages is that of their infamous wayward son who gave the family so much agony and shame. The entry relating to William's birth has been cut out of the register's relevant page and the vacant space filled with glued-on blank paper. 'Who knows who did this?' says Nico Tyack, documentation officer at the Museum of Edinburgh where the Bible now rests in the city council's special history collection. 'But it's a fair bet that it was one of the family.'

It's a fair bet, too, that that this would have been done just after the Deacon's trial and execution in 1788, six years after his father's death. His father's death was recorded in the 15cm thick leatherbound volume by Jean, William Brodie's sister who kept house for the Deacon, while his other sister Jacobina kept herself busy being the wife of local upholsterer Matthew Sheriff. She was recorded as having died in 1839.

The 50cm × 30cm volume is a fine, leather-bound copy of the Folio edition of the Holy Bible, including the King James versions of the metrical psalms. It was printed by the famous Edinburgh printer James Watson in 1722 and, after a 'lost' period, was 'discovered' and acquired in the following century by bookseller Richard Cameron – who, doing what booksellers tend to do, sold it to the city council in 1904. Since then it has been protected among many other historical curiosities in the museum's Huntley House home towards the foot of the Royal Mile.

'It is allowed out only for special occasions,' says Mr Tyack, 'as we are quite nervous about putting any of our vulnerable paper documents on permanent display. We have James Craig's original plan for the New Town, for instance, but we allow in into the light for viewing by the public only two hours per day.'

The Brodie Bible's most recent outing was on show to the public under a glass case in Edinburgh's City Art Centre as recently as July 2014. 'It is rather a sad book,' says Mr Tyack, 'not just because of the conspicuous absence of William but because of the high incidence of infant deaths within the family.' Anyone who wishes to view it can do so by making an appointment with the museum's history department.

The following two entries sit at the top of the page, where the William Brodie entry is now represented only by a blank space:

Edinburgh, the 17 August 1718, was born betwixt 11 and 12 at night, Cicel Grant (now my Spouse) Daughter to William Grant, Writer, and Jean Broun, his 2nd spouse, and was baptized nixt day by the Reveredn Mr Freebairn, in presence of the above Ludovick Brodie, John Grant and Allexander Gordon, Writers &c., named after Mrs Cicel Rentoun, Sister to the Laird of Lamerton.

Edinburgh, 20 October 1740. We the above Francis Brodie and Cecil Grant was married in Her Father's house by the Reverend Mr Wallace, Minister in Edg. Before these witnesses, viz., our two fathers John, Joseph, and Hellen Brodie's my Brother'sand Sister, Ludovick Allexander, and Jean Grant's her Brother's and Sister, and John Grant, Writer to the Signet, my Uncle and her Cousin.

[THE BLANK AREA, where there were once probably seven lines about the couple's first son; lines that were no doubt infused with joy].

Edinburgh the 22 September, 1742, was born att 6 in the morning being Wednesday, our Second Son, and deied about 11 oclock that Forenoon and was buried that evening in the Greyfriars Church Yard, two double paces to the west side of the narrow road opposite to Harley's Tomb, where a Great many of his Relations are interred.

BIBLIOGRAPHY

Helpful reading on Deacon Brodie:

Traditions of Edinburgh, Robert Chalmers (Chambers, 1940)

Kay's Edinburgh Portraits, James Paterson (Hamilton, Adams, 1885)

The Strange Case of Deacon Brodie, Forbes Bramble (Hamish Hamilton, 1975)

Deacon Brodie: Father to Jekyll and Hyde, John S Gibson (Paul Harris, 1977)

The Trial of Deacon Brodie, William Roughead (various, 1906)

Stevenson, Jekyll, Hyde and all the Deacon Brodies, Owen Dudley Edwards (NLS, 2000)

Robert Louis Stevenson, James Pope Hennessy (Jonathan Cape, 1974)

The Life of Robert Louis Stevenson, Thomas Graham Balfour (Methuen, 1901)

The RL Stevenson Originals, E B Simpson (T.N. Foulis, 1912)

The Fabulous Originals, Irving Wallace (Longmans, Green, 1955)

INDEX

Visit our website and discover thousands of
other History Press books.

www.thehistorypress.co.uk